FATHER

AN ANTHOLOGY OF VERSE

Collected and Arranged by

MARGERY DOUD

and

CLEO M. PARSLEY

Chief and First Assistant,
Readers' Advisory Service,
St. Louis Public Library

New York

E. P. DUTTON & CO., INC.

Publishers

INTRODUCTION

POEMS about Father and tributes to him are so scattered as to give the impression that little in praise of Father has been written. The purpose of this volume is to bring together certain of these poems and tributes for use on Father's Day and on such other occasions during the year as Fathers-and-Sons and Fathers-and-Daughters banquets. Although the selections included have been grouped to facilitate their use for special occasions, it is hoped that the volume as a whole will have a genuine appeal for Father himself.

Many persons are still unaware that a special day has been set aside for honoring Father, and that the distinction of having founded Father's Day belongs to Mrs. John Bruce Dodd of Spokane, Washington. Mrs. Dodd conceived the idea as a tribute to her own father, William J. Smart, who reared his motherless family alone, and in 1910 she, with two others, petitioned the Spokane Ministerial Association asking support in establishing the day. This petition, approved by the association, reads:

"The beautiful custom of Mother's Day suggests the question, Why not a Father's Day? This question is further emphasized by the celebration in our Sunday schools of Children's Day.

A Father's Day would call attention to such constructive teachings from the pulpit as would naturally point out:

The father's place in the home.

The training of children.

The safeguarding of the marriage tie.

The protection of womanhood and childhood.

The meaning of this, whether in the light of religion or of patriotism, is so apparent as to need no argument in behalf of such a day.

Your petitioners therefore urge you to set apart the third Sunday of June to be known as Father's Day, and suggest the use of the rose as a suitable flower.

Respectfully submitted,

Mrs. J. B. Dodd,
Mark H. Wheeler,
Geo. A. Forbes."

The Y.M.C.A. in the Western states supported the idea, the newspapers gave it publicity and gradually the movement spread throughout the country until Father's Day is now widely celebrated on the third Sunday in June. Greeting cards, gifts, special sermons and services emphasize the occasion. In some places a red rose is worn to honor a living father while a white one is chosen in memory of one who is dead.

M.D.
C.M.P.

ACKNOWLEDGMENT

THE compilers are most grateful to the publishers, the editors of the magazines, and the individual poets for permission to reprint the selections that comprise this Anthology. For their interest and suggestions the compilers are indebted to Arthur E. Bostwick and Harlan Eugene Read.

CONTENTS

INDEX OF AUTHORS

xi

I
FATHERS

TO MY FATHER

I

You rhymed like Lear for us when we were small.
Our walks with you were full of things mysterious
Made magic by your twinkle and half-drawl,
Because we could not tell if you were serious.
You rose to some occasions quite imperious,
"Explained" the jokes to us in comic papers,
And read us Russian fairy-tales, the shapers
Of visions grim, fantastic, and delirious.

You laughed at us and teased us and regarded
Our mediaeval lives with understanding;
And often there were monsters that you warded
Away with words unique and mirth-commanding.
We'd hang across the landing till we'd fall,
Waiting to hear your step down in the hall.

II

"Well, bears!" or "How is Little John tonight?"
"The man who made this match, my son, must be a—"
"Oh, Father, you'll not *please* turn on the light
Until we hear what happened to Gackelea!"
"Dark? Nonsense! Read? A very strange idea!"
The leather chair at last denounced this attitude,
And, coiled at various lengths, we breathed beatitude
Before some world's-end castle on Mount Moria.

There, at endearing sprawl that never cost your
True dignity the loss of one iota,
We would regard you from precarious posture,

1

Squirming with exclamation points, or stilly
As a hushed mouse, while thrillingly you'd quote a
Rhyme, or wake fairies in a tiger-lily.

III

Time, the dark whale, spouts blithely from his spiracle
A jet of memory that makes glad the sun.
In you the intuition for true fun
Wrought us the breathless and quotidian miracle.
You taught us words like these with pomp satirical,
And I have but to listen and I hear
Your voice croon, "Shed no tear, oh shed no tear!"
Swayed between the ironic and the lyrical.

Hard lines in Caesar, equations in quadratics,
Charades, acrostics, walks that made us pant
And sit on stones because our breath was scant
And our legs short; the furbishings from attics,
Furniture, daily bread, child-grief that stings,
You took, transformed, and made amazing things.

IV

Yet you have looked, even as all men must,
On the Medusa, and looked down her eyes.
Now I perceive it, in my time made wise
Though not with half the valor or the trust;
Your spirit blue as steel unflecked by rust,
Your mind forever snapping dragon-flies
Whimsical at their sheen, their sting of lies
But relish, where so soon all things are dust.

You held life to us like a twirling prism
Nor flinched a facet with your curious gaze.

You said, "Yes, so it sparkles, so it sways."
You hated, loved and smiled. No syllogism
Had said the last. All ways you cast your looks
And walked the world and read a thousand books.

v

You had the touch, the gesture, the exact
Quick divination for a thing well-said.
Sometimes I only find in what you read
To us your overtones, that drove the fact
Of greatness home with thrust, that thrid close-packed
And marvelous Browning with a tongue in cheek,
Thrilled to him on his heights, enjoyed his Greek,
And so took all the gods, with spacious tact.

Your detestation inchoate Carlyle
Turned Prussian-blue; your weakness, Stevenson.
("They" call it weakness!) In the lucky-bag
Of literature you angled, for a while
Parceled the patchwork, when the day was done
Knew every banner from every bogus rag.

VI

You found a quartz-stone, Duty, and you found
A white lamp, Truth, and Honor, a sweet fire,
Whose ways are up the jagged crags that tire
But whose domain has azure for a ground
Where trumpets snarl no more but golden sound
Hangs rapt like the great ending of a song.
There you have peers. There all your years belong
Who took that road, slung with a magic lyre.

Your hands would never touch it, but in shade
Of your proud thoughts, your dreams, to children's ears

What men will never know, but the heart hears
And sees bright-meteored mount the frowning years,
All of itself, all of itself it played
That high fantastic tune your spirit made!
                    —WILLIAM ROSE BENÉT

Reprinted from *Moons of Grandeur*, by William Rose Benét, by permission of the author.

*

MY FATHER

My father was a tall man and yet the ripened rye
Would come above his shoulders, the spears shot up so
  high.

My father was a tall man and yet the tasseled corn
Would hide him when he cut the stalks upon a frosty
  morn.

The green things grew so lushly in the valley of my birth,
Where else could one witness the luxuriance of earth?

The plow would turn so rhythmically the loose, unfettered
  loam,
There was no need of effort to drive the coulter home.

My father walked behind his team before the sun was high,
Fine as a figure on a frieze cut sharp against the sky.

And when he swung the cradle in the yellow of the grain,
He could command all eyes around, or when he drove the
  wain.

I wonder if his acres now that lie so far away
Are waiting for his footprint at the coming of the day.

I wonder if the brown old barn that still is standing long
And ghostly cattle in the stalls are waiting for his song.

—JESSIE B. RITTENHOUSE

This poem from *The Secret Bird* by Jessie B. Rittenhouse is used by
permission of, and by special arrangement with, Houghton Mifflin
Company, the authorized publishers.

*

A MAN

(*To my father*)

Often, when I would sit, a dreamy, straight-haired
        child,
A book held gaping on my knee,
Watering a sterile romance with my thoughts,
You would come bounding to the curb
And startle me to life.
You sat so straight upon your vibrant horse—
That lovely horse, all silken fire and angry grace—
And yet you seemed so merged in him,
So like! At least my thoughts
Gave you a measure of that wildness.
And oh, for many years you seemed to me
Something to marvel at and yet to fear.

But now I know that you resemble most
That growth in nature that you most revere.
You are so like, so very like, a tree—
Grown straight and strong and beautiful,

With many leaves.
The years but add in richness to your boughs,
You make a noble pattern on the sky.
About your rugged trunk
Vines creep and lichens cling,
And children play at tag.
Upon your branches some will hang their load
And rest and cool while you must brave the sun.
But you put forth new life with every year,
And tower nearer to the clouds
And never bend or grow awry.

I wonder what sweet water bathes your roots,
And if you gain your substance from the earth;
Or if you have a treaty with the sun,
Or keep some ancient promise with the heavens.

—Jean Starr Untermeyer

From *Growing Pains* by Jean Starr Untermeyer, New York, The
Viking Press, Inc. Copyright, 1918, B. W. Huebsch.

*

ONLY A DAD

Only a dad, with a tired face,
Coming home from the daily race,
Bringing little of gold or fame,
To show how well he has played the game,
But glad in his heart that his own rejoice
To see him come, and to hear his voice.

Only a dad, with a brood of four,
One of ten million men or more.

Plodding along in the daily strife,
Bearing the whips and the scorns of life,
With never a whimper of pain or hate,
For the sake of those who at home await.

Only a dad, neither rich nor proud,
Merely one of the surging crowd
Toiling, striving from day to day,
Facing whatever may come his way,
Silent, whenever the harsh condemn,
And bearing it all for the love of them.

Only a dad, but he gives his all
To smooth the way for his children small,
Doing, with courage stern and grim,
The deeds that his father did for him.
This is the line that for him I pen,
Only a dad, *but the best of men.*

—EDGAR A. GUEST

From *Heap O' Livin',* by Edgar A. Guest. Copyright, 1916, by Reilly & Lee, and reprinted by permission of the publishers.

BOOK-LOVER

My Pop is *always* buying books:
So that Mom says his study looks
        Just like an old book store.
The book shelves are so full and tall
They hide the paper on the wall,
        And there are books just everywhere,
        On table, window seat, and chair,
And books right on the floor.

And every little while he buys
More books, and brings them home and tries
To find a place where they will fit,
And has an awful time of it.

Once when I asked him *why* he got
So many books, he said, "Why not?"
I've puzzled over that a lot.

—RALPH BERGENGREN

*

A STORY OF SELF-SACRIFICE

Pop took me to the circus 'cause it disappoints me so
To have to stay at home, although he doesn't care to go;
He's seen it all so many times, the wagons and the tents;
The cages of wild animals and herds of elephants;
This morning he went down with me to watch the big
      parade,
He was so dreadful busy that he oughtn't to have stayed,
He said he'd seen it all before and all the reason he
Went down and watched it coming was because it's new
      to me.

Then we walked to the circus grounds and Pop he says:
      "I guess
You want a glass of lemonade, of course," and I says:
      "Yes."
And he bought one for each of us, and when he drank
      his he

Told me he drank it only just to keep me company;
And then he says, "The sideshow is, I s'pose, the same old
     sell,
But everybody's goin' in, so we might just as well."
He said he'd seen it all before, and all the reason he
Went in and saw it was because it was all new to me.

Well, by and by we both came out and went in the big
     tent,
And saw the lions and tigers and the bigges' elephant
With chains on his front corner and an awful funny nose
That looks around for peanuts that the crowd of people
     throws;
And Pop, he bought some peanuts and it curled its nose
     around
Until it found most every one that he threw on the
     ground;
He said he'd seen it all before, and all the reason he
Stayed there and threw 'em was because it was all new
     to me.

Well, then the band began to play the liveliestest tune,
And Pop, he says he guessed the show would open pretty
     soon;
So we went in the other tent, and Pop, he says to me:
"I guess we'll get some reserved seats so you will surely
     see."
And then some lovely ladies came and stood there on the
     ground,
And jumped up on the horses while the horses ran
     around;
Pop said he'd seen it all before, and all the reason he
Looked at the ladies was because it was all new to me.

Well, finally it's over, but a man came out to say
That they're going to have a concert, and Pop said we'd
    better stay;
He said they're always just the same and always such a
    sell,
But lots of folks was staying and he guessed we might
    as well.
Then by and by we're home again, and Mamma wants
    to know
What kind of circus was it, and Pop said, "The same
    old show,"
And said he'd seen it all before and all the reason he
Had stayed and seen it all was 'cause it's all so new to
    me.

—JAMES W. FOLEY

From *Boys and Girls,* by James W. Foley. Copyright, 1913, by E. P. Dutton & Co., Inc.

*

DADDY

When Daddy shaves and lets me stand and look,
I like it better than a picture-book.
He pulls such lovely faces all the time
Like funny people in a pantomime.

—ROSE FYLEMAN

From *Fairies and Friends,* by Rose Fyleman. Copyright, 1926, by Doubleday, Doran and Company, Inc.

AN UNUSUAL CHUM

Henry Blake's father goes fishing with him,
And goes in the creek so's to teach him to swim;
He talks to him just like they're awful close chums
And sometimes at night he helps Henry do sums;
And once he showed Henry how he used to make
A basket by whittling a peach stone and take
The bark off of willows for whistles although
He hadn't made one since a long time ago.

Henry Blake's father is just like his chum,
And when he goes fishing he lets Henry come;
He fixes two seats on the bank of the brook
And shows Henry how to put frogs on his hook; ·
And sometimes he laughs in the jolliest way
At some little thing that he hears Henry say,
And dips up a drink in his hat like you do
When only just boys go a-fishing with you.

Henry Blake's father will take him and stay
Somewhere in the woods for a half holiday
And wear his old clothes and bring home a big sack
Of hick'ries and walnuts to help Henry crack;
And sit on a dead log somewhere in the shade
To eat big sandwiches his mother has made;
And Henry Blake's father, he don't seem as though,
He's more than his uncle, he likes Henry so!

—JAMES W. FOLEY

From *Boys and Girls*, by James W. Foley. Copyright, 1913, by
E. P. Dutton & Co., Inc.

WHEN PA WAS A BOY

I wish 'at I'd of been here when
    My paw he was a boy;
They must of been excitement then—
    When my paw was a boy.
In school he always took the prize,
He used to lick boys twice his size—
I bet folks all had bulgin' eyes
    When my paw was a boy!

There was a lot of wonders done
    When my paw was a boy;
How grandpa must have loved his son,
    When my paw was a boy!
He'd git the coal and chop the wood,
And think up every way he could   .
To always just be sweet and good—
    When my paw was a boy!

Then everything was in its place,
    When my paw was a boy;
How he could rassle, jump and race,
    When my paw was a boy!
He never, never disobeyed;
He beat in every game he played—
Gee! What a record there was made!
    When my paw was a boy!

I wish 'at I'd of been here when
    My paw he was a boy;
They'll never be his like agen—
    Paw was the moddle boy.

But still last night I heard my maw
Raise up her voice and call my paw
The biggest goose she ever saw—
     He ought of stayed a boy.
                    —SAMUEL ELLSWORTH KISER

From *Ballads of the Busy Days,* by Samuel Ellsworth Kiser. Copyright, 1903, and reprinted by permission of the author.

*

EPITAPH ON MY FATHER

O ye, whose cheek the tear of pity stains,
     Draw near with pious rev'rence, and attend!
Here lie the loving husband's dear remains,
     The tender father, and the gen'rous friend.

The pitying heart that felt for human woe,
     The dauntless heart that fear'd no human pride,
The friend of man—to vice alone a foe;
     For 'ev'n his failings lean'd to virtue's side.'
                    —ROBERT BURNS

*

DADDY KNOWS

Let us dry our tears now, laddie,
     Let us put aside our woes;
Let us go and talk to daddy,
     For I'm sure that daddy knows.

Let us take him what we've broken,
　　Be it heart or hope or toy,
And the tale may bide unspoken,
　　For he used to be a boy.

He has been through all the sorrows
　　Of a lad at nine or ten;
He has seen the dawn of morrows
　　When the sun shone bright again;
His own heart has been near breaking,
　　Oh, more times than I can tell,
And has often known the aching
　　That a boy's heart knows so well.

I am sure he well remembers,
　　In his calendar of days,
When the boy-heart was December's,
　　Though the sun and flowers were May's.
He has lived a boy's life, laddie,
　　And he knows just how it goes;
Let us go and talk to daddy,
　　For I'm sure that daddy knows.

Let us tell him all about it,
　　How the sting of it is there,
And I have not any doubt it
　　Will be easier to bear;
For he's trodden every byway,
　　He has fathomed every joy,
He has traveled every highway
　　In the wide world of a boy.

He will put aside the worries
　　That his day may follow through,

For the great heart of him hurries
    At the call for help from you.
He will help us mend the broken
    Heart of ours or hope or toy,
And the tale may bide unspoken—
    For he used to be a boy.

           —JAMES W. FOLEY

From *Boys and Girls,* by James W. Foley. Copyright, 1913, by E. P. Dutton & Co., Inc.

*

HE THINKS OF HIS CHILDREN

By Hittan of Tayyi (date unknown)

Fortune has brought me down—her wonted way—
    from station great and high to low estate;
Fortune has rent away my plenteous store:
    of all my wealth honor alone is left.
Fortune has turned my joy to tears: how oft
    did fortune make me laugh with what she gave!
But for these girls, the kata's downy brood,
    unkindly thrust from door to door as hard—
Far would I roam and wide to seek my bread
    in earth that has no lack of breadth and length.
Nay, but our children in our midst, what else
    but our hearts are they, walking on the ground?
If but the breeze blow harsh on one of them
    my eye says no to slumber all night long.

        —SIR CHARLES LYALL, *Translator*

From *Ancient Arabian Poetry,* translated by Sir Charles Lyall, and reprinted by permission of The Columbia University Press of New York and Williams & Norgate Ltd. of London.

YOUR DAD

You know your dad as a big, big, man;
A marvelous being that's most like God—
A being built on a splendid plan;
Who holds the world at his beck and nod.
The happiest dream you ever dream
Is to be like him when you've older grown.
And you love to swagger and strut, and seem
To wield his power as though your own.

I know your dad as a big, big, boy—
A lovable fellow who clearly knows
How shallow the gold 'neath his soul's alloy,
And who prays: "As my manikin older grows
May he be wiser than I have been—
This lad of mine that I love so well!"
For he loves you, son, as he can't begin
In a million of lives like this, to tell.

You know your dad, and I know him too.
He needs to be known as both of us know.
The worship that comes from the heart of you
Makes all that is best in him glow and grow.
This knowledge of mine, as men know men,
That allows for failings we all deplore,
Will encourage him always to try again
That he may deserve your worship, more.

—STRICKLAND GILLILAN

From *Laugh It Off*, by Strickland Gillilan. Copyright, 1924, by Forbes & Co.

WE AIN'T SCARED O' PA

Us boys ain't scared o' Pa so much,
        He only makes a noise,
An' says he never did see such
        Onmanageable boys.
But when Ma looks around I see
        Just somethin' long an' flat
An' always make a point to be
        Some better after that.

Pa promises an' promises,
        But never does a thing;
But what Ma says she does she does,
        An' when I go to bring
Her slipper or her hair brush when
        She says she'll dust my pants,
I think I could be better then
        If I had one more chance.

Pa always says nex' time 'at he
        Will have a word to say,
But Ma she is more apt to be
        A-doin' right away;
Pa turns around at us an' glares
        As fierce as he can look,
But when we're out o' sight, upstairs,
        He goes back to his book.

Ma doesn't glare as much as Pa
        Or make as big a fuss,
But what she says is law is law,
        And when she speaks to us

She's lookin' carelessly around
  F'r somethin' long an' flat,
And when we notice it, we're bound
  To be good after that.

So we ain't scairt o' Pa at all,
  Although he thinks we are;
But when we hear Ma come an' call,
  No difference how far
We are away we answer quick,
  An' tell her where we're at,
When she stoops down and starts to pick
  Up somethin' long an' flat!

       —JAMES W. FOLEY

From *Boys and Girls,* by James W. Foley. Copyright, 1913, by E.
P. Dutton & Co., Inc.

*

WHAT MY FATHER WAS TO ME

I know just what my father was to me—
And is unto this day;
And so unto my boy would I as truly be
And in the selfsame way,
I honored, loved, respected him and he
Gave me his love as pay!
I pass it on unto that boy of mine
And hope and dream and pray
I may so live that he may know the fine
True things of life and may

Honor and love, respect, obey
His father in a better, nobler way
Than I did mine.

—D. G. BECHERS

From *The Job of Being a Dad,* compiled by Frank H. Cheley.
Copyright, 1923, by W. A. Wilde Company.

*

FATHER IS COMING

The clock is on the stroke of six,
    The father's work is done;
Sweep up the hearth, and mend the fire,
    And put the kettle on:
The wild night-wind is blowing cold,
'Tis dreary crossing o'er the wold.

He is crossing o'er the wold apace,
    He is stronger than the storm;
He does not feel the cold, not he,
    His heart it is so warm;
For father's heart is stout and true
As ever human bosom knew.

He makes all toil, all hardship light;
    Would all men were the same!
So ready to be pleased, so kind,
    So very slow to blame!
Folks need not be unkind, austere;
For love hath readier will than fear.

Nay, do not close the shutters, child,
    For far along the lane
The little window looks, and he
    Can see it shining plain;
I've heard him say he loves to mark
The cheerful firelight, through the dark.

And we'll do all that father likes;
    His wishes are so few;
Would they were more; that every hour
    Some wish of his I knew!
I'm sure it makes a happy day
When I can please him any way.

I know he's coming by this sign,
    That baby's almost wild,
See how he laughs, and crows, and stares—
    Heaven bless the merry child!
His father's self in face and limb,
And father's heart is strong in him.

Hark! hark! I hear his footsteps now,
    He's through the garden gate;
Run, little Bess, and ope the door,
    And do not let him wait.
Shout, baby, shout! and clap thy hands,
For father on the threshold stands.

—MARY HOWITT

From *One Thousand Poems for Children*, compiled by R. Ingpen.
Copyright, by George W. Jacobs & Co.

MARGARET ROPER'S VISION OF HER FATHER, SIR THOMAS MORE

The vision of her girlhood glinted by:—
And how the father through their garden stray'd
And, child with children, play'd
And teased the rabbit-hutch, and fed the dove
Before him from above
Alighting, in his visitation sweet,
Led on by little hands, and eager feet.

Hence among those he stands,
Elect ones, ever in whose ears the word
He that offends these little ones . . . is heard;
With love and kisses smiling-out commands,
And all the tender hearts within his hands;
Seeing, in every child that goes, a flower
From Eden's nursery bower,
A little stray from Heaven, for reverence here
Sent down, and comfort dear:
All care well paid-for by one pure caress,
And life made happy in their happiness.

—FRANCIS TURNER PALGRAVE

From his poem "London Bridge" in *Visions of England,* by Francis
Turner Palgrave. By permission of The Macmillan Company, pub-
lishers.

*

TO MY FATHER

(Sir Herbert Beerbohm Tree, 1853–1917)

I cannot think that you have gone away,
You loved the earth—and life lit up your eyes,

And flickered in your smile that would surmise
Death as a song, a poem, or a play.
You were reborn afresh with every day,
And baffled fortune in some new disguise.
Ah! can it perish when the body dies,
Such youth, such love, such passion to be gay?
We shall not see you come to us and leave
A conqueror—nor catch on fairy wing
Some slender fancy—nor new wonders weave
Upon the loom of your imagining.
The world is wearier, grown dark to grieve
Her child that was a pilgrim and a king.

—IRIS TREE

*

IN SALUTATION TO MY FATHER'S SPIRIT

(Aghorenath Chattopadhyay)

Farewell, farewell, O brave and tender Sage.
O mystic Jester, golden-hearted child!
Selfless, serene, untroubled, unbeguiled
By trivial snares of grief and greed or rage;
O splendid dreamer in a dreamless age
Whose deep alchemic vision reconciled
Time's changing message with the undefiled
Calm wisdom of thy Vedic heritage!

Farewell, great spirit, without fear of flaw,
Thy life was love and liberty thy law,
And Truth thy pure imperishable goal . . .

All hail to thee in thy transcendent flight
From hope to hope, from height to heav'nlier height,
Lost in the rapture of the Cosmic Soul.

—SAROJINI NAIDU

From *The Sceptered Flute,* by Sarojini Naidu. Copyright, 1928, by Dodd, Mead & Company, Inc., and used by their permission.

*

FLIGHT OF CROWS

(In memoriam W.J.L. 1837–1920)

I

Out of the chaos of sunset, the one white star and silence,
    Far in the fiery dusk, off at the ends of the world,
Out of the lavender twilight of misty October horizons,
    Bursts, like a birth in the skies, swarming the legion
    of crows;
Onward and over the valley, and strangely perturbed in
    their winging
    Bigger and blacker they stream, cawing in answer
    to caw.
So have I noted in April the wild-geese honking to north-
    ward,
    Only in loftier air, up in the blue and the day . . .
Morning and night and the seasons, and ever the ancient
    migrations,
    While, for his hour, a man . . . stands on a hill
    as they pass.

II

News, like the caw of the crow or the cry of the Canada
    flyers,
    Startled me walking at noon, naming me one who
        had died—
Flashed by the desolate wires that yonder, threading the
    tree-tops
    Pole unto pole on the moor, under the flight of the
        crows,
Still are to see, on a silvery strip of the nethermost
    heavens,
    Cutting the splotches of red, crossing from darkness
        to dark . . .
News of the earth and the ages, and spelt by the spirit of
    lightning:
    Bolt from the cloud or the wire—each is an omen
        to man.

III

Here by the mound of the Eagle, obscure in the yellowing
    grasses,
    Under an oak that is gone, leaving the acorn for ours,
Once, ere the Saxon invader re-named the ravines and
    the ranges,
    Bronze hands kindled a blaze, cheery and pungent
        as mine,—
Pausing I fancy as I, while followed the last of the
    fledglings
    Bat-like hither and yon—suddenly swifter away . . .
Night and the seasons and cycles, and ever the ancient
    migrations,
    While, for its hour, a fire . . . burns on a hill as
    they pass.

IV

And as the haze and the gloaming have blotted the roads
    and the landmarks,
        Yonder and yonder the plain . . . spreads like an
        alien world,
Quiet, primeval and vast, as in autumns after the ice-age,
        When, from the journeying seeds, blown by the
        South in the spring
(Blown to the edge of the desert, the hollows of silt and
    the drumlins,
        Borne in the toes of a tern, cast in the dung of a
        deer),
Summer by summer the junipers, sumachs, birches, and
    berries
        Gained on the leagues to the north, bleak with
        Arcturus and cold . . .
Season and cycle and aeon, and ever the ancient migra-
    tions,
        Whether a man and his fire . . . linger or not on
        the hill.
              —WILLIAM ELLERY LEONARD

*

TO MY FATHER

As the poorest may borrow some treasure
    To adorn what is meagre or bare,
So a memory loved beyond measure
    I lay on my book, with the prayer,

Its dear presence all fault may efface,
And a lingering touch of its grace
    May ennoble my words unaware.
                    —GRACE DENIO LITCHFIELD

From *Collected Poems* by Grace Denio Litchfield, and reprinted
by permission of the author. Copyright, 1913.

*

MY WONDERFUL DAD

My Daddy, he lived in a wonderful house, and he played
    with such wonderful boys;
They were neighbors of his; and the attic they had was
    a storehouse of wonderful toys;
He slept every night in a wonderful bed, with a tick that
    his grandmother made
From the feathers of geese that she picked all herself, and
    so soft he was almost afraid
He would sink out of sight when he got into bed; he could
    look from his window right out
And see where the vines used to bring him sweet flowers
    just by crawling along up the spout;
And he could look over and see where the woods and the
    squirrels and birds used to be.
He must have had wonderful times where he lived from
    the way that he tells them to me!

My Daddy, he caught the most wonderful fish—there
    were thin ones and fat ones and round,
And some were so long that their tails when he walked
    would be dragging right down on the ground;

He scraped off their scales on a log that he had at the
    woodpile, and said he would know
That log just as well if he saw it today, although that
    was a long time ago.
He used to dig worms of a wonderful size—he has never
    seen any like those
Since he was grown up; and on Saturdays he wore a
    wonderful old suit of clothes
And a hat that an uncle of his had forgot, for on Friday
    he did all his sums,
And Saturday always he went off somewhere with his one
    or two wonderful chums.

My Daddy, he lived in a wonderful place when he was a
    twelve-year-old lad,
For no matter what kind of a day it might be there was
    always some fun to be had.
He learned how to swim in a wonderful creek, where all
    of the whole summer long
The water was warm, and the springboard they had it
    was springy and slippery and strong.
And on the way home they found berries to eat, and he
    said he remembers them well,
And it didn't seem nearly a mile to back home, for there
    always was something to tell
That took up the time both for him and his chums, and
    sometimes they came home a new way,
And always all summer they had it all planned what to do
    on the next Saturday.

My Daddy, he said he could go back there now and could
    take me as straight as a string
To all of the wonderful places he knew—where the first
    flowers came in the spring;

Where you almost were sure to catch fish in the brook—
    where the nuts would come dropping in fall;
Where the most berries were on the way to back home—
    he is sure he remembers them all.
He knows where the squirrels were most apt to be, and
    the lane where the hay wagon comes;
And said he'd find names in the bark of a tree that were
    cut there by him and his chums
Twenty-five years ago, and the log where they sat when
    they found the big garter-snake curled.
My Daddy, he must have had wonderful times in the
    splendidest place in the world!

—James W. Foley

From *Boys and Girls,* by James W. Foley. Copyright, 1913, by
E. P. Dutton & Co., Inc.

*

WHEN DADDY SINGS

When Daddy sings he keeps his chin
Pressed tight against his chest,
And just before the folks begin
He gives his voice a test,
And growls "Do, do" first high, then low,
To see which way sounds best.

When Daddy sings it makes him frown
Or wrinkle up his nose.
He waves one finger up and down
The way the music goes;
And when the song lasts very long,
He rises on his toes.

"Black Joe" and "Cradle of the Deep"—
He growls them extra strong.
I don't know why he cares a heap
To see what words belong.
He just sings "Tum ti iddy um"
In every single song.

—BURGES JOHNSON

From *Youngsters, Collected Poems of Childhood*, by Burges
Johnson. Copyright, 1921, by E. P. Dutton & Co., Inc.

*

TO MY FATHER

Nothing ever grips me,
Though I've tried Life's every lure,
The Primrose Path is but a byway,
The Narrow one but a road.
The song and wine and fruits forbidden
May so remain for aught of me,
For I succumb to my longings
And soon forget . . .
My work, my wants, my thoughts
Are but harbingers of futility,
For nothing ever grips me . . .
Nothing save the one hope
Science hasn't killed—
That when I die
We shall be pals again.

—PHILARDEE

From *Column Poets*, edited by Keith Preston. Copyright, 1924, by
Pascal Covici, and reprinted by permission of Covici, Friede Inc.

THE FINEST FELLOWSHIP

There may be finer pleasures than just tramping with
  your boy,
And better ways to spend a day; there may be sweeter joy;
There may be richer fellowship than that of son and dad,
But if there is, I know it not; it's one I've never had.

Oh, some may choose to walk with kings and men of
  pomp and pride,
But as for me, I choose to have my youngster at my side.
And some may like the rosy ways of grown-up pleasures
  glad,
But I would go a-wandering with just a little lad.

Yes, I would seek the woods with him and talk to him of
  trees,
And learn to know the birds a-wing and hear their
  melodies;
And I would drop all worldly care and be a boy awhile;
Then hand-in-hand come home at dusk to see the mother
  smile.

Grown men are wearisome at times, and selfish pleasures
  jar,
But sons and dads throughout the world the truest com-
  rades are.
So when I want a perfect day with every joy that's fine,
I spend it in the open with that little lad o' mine.

—EDGAR A. GUEST

THE WAY OF A MAN

That paper that my dad received
    Three years ago today,
Somebody run and get it quick;
    He wants it right away.
So mother looks through boxes old,
    We keep beneath the stair;
And I ransack the cabinet,
    But the paper isn't there.

Dad scolds the entire household;
    From the guiltless butler down.
And says that all the worthless stuff,
    Is just left lying round;
But everything that's valuable,
    Despite the final cost,—
Is stuck where it can not be found,
    If neither burned nor lost.

And so Dad keeps complaining,
    Until mother starts to sing,
And then he frowns in silent rage,
    And doesn't say a thing.
The house looks like a hurricane;
    Then in a fit of gloom
Small Jimmie grabs his ball and bat,
    And races from the room.

And mother thinks the paper's lost;
    And sister *knows* it's gone;
And Dad is tired of thinking
    So he scowls and just looks on.
Then mother makes a final search,

Through Father's private shelf,
And, there it is. *He* recollects,
He put it there himself.

—LOIS HALDERMAN

From *Little Book of Verse,* published 1920 by Westinghouse High
School, Pittsburgh, Pa. This poem was written while the author was
in High School, and is reprinted by her permission.

*

WHEN PAPA WAS A BOY

When papa was a little boy you really couldn't find
In all the country round about a child so quick to mind.
His mother never called but once, and he was always
    there;
He never made the baby cry or pulled his sister's hair.
He never slid down banisters or made the slightest noise,
And never in his life was known to fight with other boys.
He always rose at six o'clock and went to bed at eight,
And never lay abed till noon; and never sat up late.

He finished Latin, French and Greek when he was ten
    years old
And knew the Spanish alphabet as soon as he was told.
He never, never thought of play until his work was done,
He labored hard from break of day until the set of sun.
He never scraped his muddy shoes upon the parlor floor,
And never answered back his ma, and never banged the
    door.
"But, truly, I could never see," said little Dick Molloy,
"How he could never do these things and really be a boy."

EARL ALONZO BRININSTOOL

Reprinted by permission of the author.

POP

If a fairy should come from Babyland
With a smile on his face and a wand in his hand,
And say to me in his merry way,
"I wish to hear what you have to say
'Bout being born all over again—
Exactly where and exactly when
And just what kind of a feller you'd like
To have for your dad on this earthly hike,"

I'd look at him and try to be
As nonchalant and gay as he,
And then I'd say, "If I must be
Born again, it seems to me,
It doesn't matter much just where or when
(For what's a baby now and then?)
But there's one thing I must request
So will you do your level best

And kindly see that I shall drop
Into the self-same arms of the self-same Pop?
For, take it from me, he's the very best dad
That any baby's ever had!"

—Elinor Maxwell

From *Little Beggar and Other Poems,* by Elinor Maxwell and reprinted by permission of the author. Copyright, 1924.

*

IN THE STUDY

Nicest place in all the house
Is my poppa's study chair;

Just as quiet as a mouse
    I go creeping there,
An' he gives a little smile,
Writing, writing, all the while.

There's at least a million books
    Up and down and round the wall.
I guess, from the way it looks,
    I can't read them all!
If I did I'm sure I'd be
Just as wise and big as he.

                    —BURGES JOHNSON

From *Youngsters, Collected Poems of Childhood,* by Burges Johnson. Copyright, 1921, by E. P. Dutton & Co., Inc.

*

DAD'S BIRTHDAY

They were passing the toy-shop, his Daddy and he,
(Thus in confidence Willie explained it to me
So soon as he found me a person of sense)
And Willie had money—four new, shining pence!

He looked in the window to see if they had
The sort of a toy that might do for a Dad,
And jingled his coins, and was counting the cost
Of a train or a trumpet when—'Daddy was lost!'

Very glistening the eyes that were lifted to mine.
What was it, I wonder, that made them so shine!
If a girl's, I should guess that it might have been tears—
But Willie's a boy, a boy of six years.

And a *boy* must not cry although lost, as was he
Who that day by the toy-shop demanded of me:
'Do you know where my Daddy went?' Then by the way
Of description—'An *old* man: he's thirty to-day!'

His voice awoke another voice, insisting to be heard;
The voice that loves the impolite, unnecessary word:
'You own,' it said, 'to having passed—was it your thirty-
        third?
O what a very, very, very, venerable bird!'

                                        —ARTHUR VINE HALL

From *Poems of a South African,* by Arthur Vine Hall. Copyrght,
1926, by Longmans Green & Co., of New York and London.

                            *

THE FAMILY MAN AS A POET

My poetic fancy wanders into thoughts of measured
        rhyme
And I see my songs go marching downward thru the
        halls of time.
In an ecstasy of vision I sit down and try to write,
While my thoughts go soaring upward in a frenzy of
        delight,
But before I get them marshalled comes a baby's pleading
        cry,
"Papa, take me; I'm so sleepy." And I take her with a
        sigh.

Presently she's soundly sleeping and I lay her gently
        down;

Then I turn to my forsaken paper, forcing back a frown,
While I thrust my nervous fingers into my disheveled
hair,
Vainly hoping that I'll find my scattered thoughts re-
gathered there.
When I quiet down to thinking and I turn again to write,
Comes a childish voice and whispers, "Papa, kiss me now
good night."

All are sleeping now. The room's deserted and I fondly
count
That I'm now at peace; so truant Pegasus again I mount,
Now my fancy lingers, coming slowly, then returns again,
And the words begin to muster at the bidding of my pen.
But before a line is written comes another nervous shock,
And a voice calls sweetly downward, "Don't forget to
wind the clock."

—JOSEPH SCHUYLER LONG

Reprinted by permission of the author.

FATHER

The little son looks in the father's face
With big, blue, wondering eyes, in which we trace
Fair, hazy visions—childhood's earliest dreams.
Ah, little one! to thee thy father seems
A world of mystery; thy great desire
To be a man—in all things like thy sire.
Thou canst not comprehend him, yet thine arms
Steal softly round his neck; his whisper charms
Thy fears away. . . .

. . . O God, we gaze at Thee;
Thou art to us how vast a mystery—
Yet Father! So we come and nestle near,
For there the mystery itself is dear;
And they shall grow, who ever there abide,
Into Thy likeness, and be satisfied.

—ARTHUR VINE HALL

From *Poems of a South African,* by Arthur Vine Hall. Copyright,
1926, by Longmans Green & Co., of New York and London.

*

MY FATHER

Was it a constancy of wind that kept
His honor clean? A wind that sweeps one spot
Reduces excess ego to a dot
That isn't there; it says to all except
The babblers and the flagrantly inept
"Honor's the thing!—when honor is forgot
A man is ready to die and ready to rot!"
My father was a man the winds had swept.

His business was not law, as some suppose,
Who think a soul is made of molecules;
His business was constructing, day by day,
An immortality—for there are those
Who build it tile on tile, and there are fools
Who strenuously piddle it away!

—VIRGINIA MOORE

From *Not Poppy* by Virginia Moore. Copyright, 1926, by Harcourt,
Brace and Company, Inc.

PRAYER TO THE SUN

My Father,
Here for a moment in your light I stand,
And feel upon my lifted face
Your touch, your touch, as of a father's hand.
Shine down upon me. See,
It is so little and so brief a thing
That drinks your light, remembering
The dark that was, the dark that is to be—
So soon to be again.
O let your glance fall tenderly and mild!
Have pity now, and when
The night has taken me have pity then,
Father, on me, your child.

—JOHN HALL WHEELOCK

*

LINES TO MY FATHER

The many sow, but only the chosen reap;
Happy the wretched host if Day be brief,
That with the cool oblivion of sleep
A dawnless Night may soothe the smart of grief.

If from the soil our sweat enriches sprout
One meagre blossom for our hands to cull,
Accustomed indigence provokes a shout
Of praise that life becomes so bountiful.

Now ushered regally into your own,
Look where you will, as far as eye can see,
Your little seeds are to a fullness grown,
And golden fruit is ripe on every tree.

Yours is no fairy gift, no heritage
Without travail, to which weak wills aspire;
This is a merited and grief-earned wage
From One Who holds His servants worth their hire.

So has the shyest of your dreams come true,
Built not of sand, but of the solid rock,
Impregnable to all that may accrue
Of elemental rage: storm, stress, and shock.

—COUNTEE CULLEN

From *Copper Sun,* by Countee Cullen. Copyright, 1927, by Harper
& Brothers.

*

FATHER'S JOURNEY

He goes

When father goes to Gunjiwump
He keeps the family on a jump.
Jim hauls the wagon in the yard
To grease the axles up with lard;
He rubs the old horse down with care,
And gets the whip in good repair;
He mends the harness up with string
And makes it strong as anything;
He cleans the wheels up at the pump,

When father goes to Gunjiwump.
    He scrapes and scours for hours and hours,
And flits and flutters on the jump,
    For we all have to worry and hurry and skurry
When father goes to Gunjiwump.

When father goes to Gunjiwump
He doesn't go like any gump;
He has his boots greased up in style
With the best kind of linseed "ile."
This is the task for little Joe,
Of lamentation and of woe;
He bears on hard and rubs it in
With mutterings, which to speak were sin;
He gives the cowhides many a thump,
And hates the name of Gunjiwump.
For it just doubles our toils and troubles,
    And masses them a solid lump;
'Tis an aggregation of tribulation
    When father goes to Gunjiwump.

When father goes to Gunjiwump
They gather round him in a clump,
Matilda, Martha, Jane and Sue,
Each with some special task to do.
Matilda tries to part his hair,
Marth gets his whiskers in repair,
Jane fixes his suspenders right,
And Sue she gets his collar tight;
They fuss and fuddle on the jump
When father goes to Gunjiwump.
They fix his tackle, and coax and cackle,
    And gather round him in a clump;

They fasten and button whatever he's got on
   When father goes to Gunjiwump.

We all sink down, a helpless lump,
When father's gone to Gunjiwump;
We only lie around and shirk,
For we are all too tired to work.
But mother says, "He looked as nice
As if he had been kept on ice;
Not many young swells look so trim
And dickydandyfied as him;
To beat his get-up, I will stump
Most any dude in Gunjiwump."
Though bruised and battered, we are all flattered,
   A self-congratulating clump;
In glowing phrases we sound his praises
   When father's gone to Gunjiwump.

He comes

When father comes from Gunjiwump
He keeps the family on a jump.
Like Caesar on his triumph car,
Young Tom espies him from afar,
And jubilantly runs from home
To bid him welcome into Rome.
He spies him by the alder clump,
The conqueror from Gunjiwump.
With his trophies of candy he makes himself handy,
   And on the new drum does he joyously thump.
Like an army with banners, a host with hosannas,
   Does father come from Gunjiwump.

When father comes from Gunjiwump
We run to meet him by the pump,—
Matilda, Martha, Jane and Sue,
Each with her special hullabaloo;
And quickly scoots out from the shed
The swift and spinning form of Ned.
It seems like Gabriel with his trump
When father comes from Gunjiwump.
We fuss and flutter, and spurt and sputter,—
　　All dull, domestic duties dump;
'Tis a jubilation, a glad vacation
　　When father comes from Gunjiwump.

When father comes from Gunjiwump
We gather round him in a clump;
Matilda gets a gingham dress
To aggravate her loveliness,
Marth gets her shoes; a colored skein
Of cotton yarn for sister Jane.
For Sue and ma his pockets dump
A mighty pack from Gunjiwump.
And we spread each trophy upon the "sofy,"
　　A self-congratulating clump,
And talk and clatter, and shout and chatter,
　　When father comes from Gunjiwump.

When father comes from Gunjiwump,
He throws his clothing in a clump,
His jacket on the cellar door,
His boots and collar on the floor.
His vesture, in sad disarray,
We put to rights some time next day.
Tom says it makes the family "hump"
When father comes from Gunjiwump.

But we're glad of the worry, the hurry and skurry,
   That keeps us on the constant jump,
Each thinks of the trophy that lies on the "sofy"
   When father comes from Gunjiwump.
            —SAM WALTER FOSS

From *Back Country Poems,* by Sam Walter Foss. Copyright, 1894, by Lothrop, Lee & Shepard.

*

IF PAW COULD HAVE HIS WAY

If paw could have his way, I bet that purty sudden there
Would be some changes that would make the people stop
   and stare;
There wouldn't be no heroes then, exceptin' only paw,
And this would be the greatest world a-buddy ever saw;
They wouldn't be no bills fer gas, nor tax fer folks to pay.
And cars would just be run fer fun, if paw could have
   his way.

If paw could have his way they'd raise his wages at the
   store,
We'd never have no bother with the hired girls no more,
And every time my shoes wore out they'd be another pair
Begin to sprout right off to keep my feet from gittin' bare,
And maw, she'd set around and smile, without a word
   to say,
But only listen all the while, if paw could have his way.

If paw could only have his way, the winters would be hot,
And in the summer-time the snow would fly, I tell you
   what!

The dry spells always would be wet, the wet spells would
   be dry,
And when the sun was shinin' clouds would spread acrost
   the sky;
Then March would be October and December would be
   May.
And they'd be more Sunday mornings, too, if paw could
   have his way.

If paw could have his way, the crowds would cheer fer
   him, I bet,
And all the fashionable folks would want him in their set;
The people that we know would all have less than we had
   then,
And wouldn't leave us out when they got parties up agen!
We'd have the best house on the street and all the folks
   would say
That they'd be glad if they was us—if paw could have
   his way.

                    —SAMUEL ELLSWORTH KISER

From *Ballads of the Busy Days,* by Samuel Ellsworth Kiser. Copy-
right, 1903, and reprinted by permission of the author.

A BOY'S KING

My papa, he's the bestest man
   What ever lived, I bet,
And I ain't never seen no one
   As smart as he is yet.
Why, he knows everything, almost,
   But mamma says that he

Ain't never been the President,
　　And that surprises me.

And often papa talks about
　　How he must work away—
He's got to toil for other folks
　　And do what others say;
And that's a thing that bothers me—
　　When he's so good and great,
He ought, I think, at least to be
　　The Ruler of the State!

He knows the names of lots of stars,
　　And he knows all the trees,
And he can tell the different kinds
　　Of all the birds he sees,
And he can multiply and add
　　And figure in his head—
They might have been some smarter men
　　But I bet you they are dead.

Once when he thought I wasn't near
　　He talked to mamma then
And told her how he hates to be
　　The slave of other men,
And how he wished that he was rich
　　For her and me—and I
Don't know what made me do it, but
　　I had to go and cry!

And so when I sat on his knee
　　I ast him: "Is it true
That you're a slave and have to toil
　　When others tell you to?

You are so big and good and wise,
    You surely ought to be
The President, instead of just
    A slave, it seems to me."

And then the tears come in his eyes,
    He hugged me tight and said:—
"Why, no, my dear, I'm not a slave—
    What put that in your head?
I am a king—the happiest king
    That ever yet held sway,
And only God can take my throne
    And little realm away!"
           —SAMUEL ELLSWORTH KISER

*

A LAST JOURNEY

"Father, you seem to have been sleeping fair?"
The child uncovered the dimity-curtained window-square
    And looked out at the dawn,
    And back at the dying man nigh gone,
    And propped up in his chair,
Whose breathing a robin's "chink" took up in antiphon.

    The open fireplace spread
    Like a vast weary yawn above his head,
Its thin blue blower waved against his whitening crown,
    For he could not lie down:
He raised him on his arms so emaciated:—

"Yes; I've slept long, my child. But as for rest,
    Well, that I cannot say.
The whole night have I footed field and turnpike-way—
    A regular pilgrimage—as at my best
        And very briskest day!

" 'Twas first to Weatherb'ry, to see them there,
    And thence to King's-Stag, where
I joined in a jolly trip to Weydon-Priors Fair:
    I shot for nuts, bought gingerbreads, cream-cheese;
        And, not content with these,
I went to London: heard the watchmen cry the hours.

"I soon was off again, and found me in the bowers
    Of father's apple-trees,
And he shook the apples down: they fell in showers,
Whereon he turned, smiled strange at me, as ill at ease;
    And then you pulled the curtain; and, ah me,
        I found me back where I wished not to be!"

'Twas told the child next day: "Your father's dead."
    And, struck, she questioned, "O,
That journey, then, did father really go?—
Buy nuts, and cakes, and travel at night till dawn was red,
    And tire himself with journeying, as he said,
        To see those old friends that he cared for so?"

                                        —THOMAS HARDY

From *Collected Poems,* by Thomas Hardy. By permission of The
Macmillan Company, publishers.

A MAN

(For My Father)

I listened to them talking, talking,
That tableful of keen and clever folk,
Sputtering . . . followed by a pale and balking
Sort of flash whenever some one spoke;
Like musty fireworks or a pointless joke,
Followed by a pointless, musty laughter. Then
Without a pause, the sputtering once again . . .
The air was thick with epigrams and smoke;
And underneath it all
It seemed that furtive things began to crawl,
Hissing and striking in the dark,
Aiming at no particular mark,
And careless whom they hurt.
The petty jealousies, the smiling hates
Shot forth their venom as they passed the plates,
And hissed and struck again, aroused, alert;
Using their feeble smartness as a screen
To shield their poisonous stabbing, to divert
From what was cowardly and black and mean.

Then I thought of you,
Your gentle soul,
Your large and quiet kindness;
Ready to caution and console,
And, with an almost blindness
To what was mean and low.
Baseness you never knew;
You could not think that falsehood was untrue,
Nor that deceit would ever dare betray you.
You even trusted treachery; and so,

Guileless, what guile or evil could dismay you?
You were for counsels rather than commands.
Your sweetness was your strength, your strength a sweet-
      ness
That drew all men, and made reluctant hands
Rest long upon your shoulder.
Firm, but never proud,
You walked your sixty years as through a crowd
Of friends who loved to feel your warmth, and who
Knowing that warmth, knew you.
Even the casual beholder
Could see your fresh and generous completeness,
Like dawn in a deep forest, growing and shining through.
Such faith has soothed and armed you. It has smiled
Frankly and unashamed at Death; and, like a child,
Swayed half by joy and half by reticence,
Walking beside its nurse, you walk with Life;
Protected by your smile and an immense
Security and simple confidence.

Hearing the talkers talk, I thought of you . . .
And it was like a great wind blowing
Over confused and poisonous places.
It was like sterile spaces
Crowded with birds and grasses, soaked clear through
With sunlight, quiet and vast and clean.
And it was forests growing,
And it was black things turning green.
And it was laughter on a thousand faces . . .
It was, like victory rising from defeat,
The world made well again and strong—and sweet.

                              —LOUIS UNTERMEYER

II

FATHERS AND SONS

SECRET LAUGHTER

There is a secret laughter
    That often comes to me,
And though I go about my work
As humble as can be,
There is no prince or prelate
    I envy—no, not one.
No evil can befall me—
    By God, I have a son!
        —CHRISTOPHER MORLEY

THE FATHER

Come with me then, my son;
    Thine eyes are wide for truth:
And I will give thee memories,
    And thou shalt give me youth.

The lake laps in silver,
    The streamlet leaps her length:
And I will give thee wisdom,
    And thou shalt give me strength.

The mist is on the moorland,
    The rain roughs the reed:

53

And I will give thee patience,
　　And thou shalt give me speed.

When lightnings lash the skyline
　　Then thou shalt learn thy part:
And when the heav'ns are direst,
　　For thee to give me heart.

Forthrightness I will teach thee;
　　The vision and the scope;
To hold the hand of honour :—
　　And thou shalt give me hope;

And when the heav'ns are deepest
　　And stars most bright above;
May God then teach thee duty;
　　And thou shalt teach me love.

　·　　·　　·　　·　　·　　·　　·

—SIR RONALD ROSS

From *Poems,* by Sir Ronald Ross. Reprinted by permission of the
publishers, Elkin Mathews & Marrot, Ltd., London, and the author.

*

TO A CERTAIN LITTLE BOY

When you are really quite grown up,
Too big to drain this little cup,
I hope the gods are kind, my boy,
And fill Life's cup with magic joy.

I pray that from a golden bowl
You may drink wisdom for your soul,
And in the chalice of the years
Find much of peace, and less of tears;
Find knowledge, beauty, faith, and love,
And every blessing from above;
But most of all, in goodly share,
Yourself pour Human Kindness there.

—CHARLES HANSON TOWNE

From *Today and Tomorrow,* by Charles Hanson Towne. Copyright,
1916, Doubleday, Doran and Company, Inc.

*

INSCRIPTION FOR MY LITTLE SON'S SILVER PLATE

When thou dost eat from off this plate,
I charge thee be thou temperate;
Unto thine elders at the board
Do thou sweet reverence accord;
And, though to dignity inclined,
Unto the serving-folk be kind;
Be ever mindful of the poor,
Nor turn them hungry from the door;
And unto God, for health and food
And all that in thy life is good,
Give thou thy heart in gratitude.

—EUGENE FIELD

From *Poems,* by Eugene Field. Copyright, 1926, by Charles Scrib-
ner's Sons, and reprinted by their permission.

MY SON STANDS ALONE

Suddenly, as you are clinging to my hands
With the accustomed clutch, I see a light
Blaze in your eyes. Your brows draw taut. Your feet
Patter for purchase. And your tongue thrusts earward.
Then valiantly you sway away from me. . . .

There is a weight pressing upon my heart.
One moment more, and you will cease to be
The funny, creeping, horizontal Something
Which never has won the perpendicular
Save as some small attachment, propped and guarded. . . .

Now . . . you will be a unit—and erect!

I thrust aside the fat solemnities
That crowd my thought; the pity and the longing
To spare you from the fight that you must make,
Ever and always, merely not to lose
The rudiments of the upright position—
The stumblings, and the fallings, and the bruises
That will be yours, until the ultimate hour
That crowns the victory of the Horizontal. . . .

But see! Your fingers lift, your body tilts
Backward—your arms are tiny, quivering wings—
The air rings with the gurgling, triumphant
Lilt of your laughter—
      And you stand—alone!

                         —JOHN V. A. WEAVER

From *Turning Point* by John V. A. Weaver. By permission of and special arrangement with Alfred A. Knopf, Inc., authorized publishers.

A PARENTAL ODE TO MY SON, AGED THREE YEARS AND FIVE MONTHS

Thou happy, happy elf!
(But stop,—first let me kiss away that tear)—
Thou tiny image of myself!
(My love, he's poking peas into his ear!)
Thou merry, laughing sprite!
With spirits feather-light,
Untouch'd by sorrow and unsoil'd by sin—
(Good heavens! the child is swallowing a pin!)

Thou little tricksy Puck!
With antic toys so funnily bestuck,
Light as the singing bird that wings the air—
(The door! the door! he'll tumble down the stair!)
Thou darling of thy sire!
(Why, Jane, he'll set his pinafore a-fire!)
Thou imp of mirth and joy!
In love's dear chain so strong and bright a link,
Thou idol of thy parents—(Drat the boy!
There goes my ink!)

Thou cherub—but of earth;
Fit playfellow for Fays, by moonlight pale,
In harmless sport and mirth,
(That dog will bite him if he pulls its tail!)
Thou human humming-bee, extracting honey
From ev'ry blossom in the world that blows,
Singing in Youth's Elysium ever sunny—
(Another tumble!—that's his precious nose!)

Thy father's pride and hope!
(He'll break the mirror with that skipping-rope!)

With pure heart newly stamp'd from Nature's mint—
(Where *did* he learn that squint?)
        Thou young domestic dove!
(He'll have that jug off, with another shove!)
        Dear nursling of the hymeneal nest!
        (Are those torn clothes his best!)
        Little epitome of man!
(He'll climb upon the table, that's his plan!)
Touch'd with the beauteous tints of dawning life—
        (He's got a knife!)

        Thou enviable being!
No storms, no clouds, in thy blue sky foreseeing,
        Play on, play on,
        My elfin John!
Toss the light ball—bestride the stick—
(I knew so many cakes would make him sick!)
With fancies buoyant as the thistledown,
Prompting the face grotesque, and antic brisk,
        With many a lamb-like frisk—
(He's got the scissors, snipping at your gown!)

        Thou pretty opening rose!
(Go to your mother, child, and wipe your nose!)
Balmy, and breathing music like the South,
(He really brings my heart into my mouth!)
Fresh as the morn, and brilliant as its star,—
(I wish that window had an iron bar!)
Bold as the hawk, yet gentle as the dove—
        (I'll tell you what, my love,
I cannot write, unless he's sent above!)

                                    —THOMAS HOOD

FOR A VERY LITTLE BOY

Your eyes are sea-blue, and they hold
New visions they will not unfold.

You laugh and cry and sleep and play
And eat and croon each lazy day.

Your hours are dreams and happiness,
And life, your mother's warm caress.

You know not 'neath the singing skies
Are hurt tears and shame and lies.

You think 'tis Heaven you are in.
You know not trouble, care, nor sin.

Oh, Baby, may you never know
The sordid things, the mean, the low.

But should they come, the things we dread,
Then—God's own blessing on your head.

—EDMUND LEAMY

From *Good Housekeeping,* October, 1922.

*

THE BIRTHDAY

A laughing, panting little Pan,
   A happy Pete on his fourth birthday,
Dropping his arms of golden tan,

Solemn a moment, suddenly ran
    Back to his play.

Then, "What's the matter?" said Pete to me,
    Hearing me laugh, hearing me sigh . . .
"I'm not so young as I used to be,"
I answered—and quick as a bird said he,
    "Neither am I!"

                                        —WITTER BYNNER

From *Grenstone Poems,* by Witter Bynner. By permission of and
special arrangement with Alfred A. Knopf, Inc., authorized publishers.

*

NOT A CHILD

I

"Not a child: I call myself a boy,"
Says my king, with accent stern yet mild,
Now nine years have brought him change of joy;
    "Not a child."

How could reason be so far beguiled,
Err so far from sense's safe employ,
Stray so wide of truth, or run so wild?

Seeing his face bent over book or toy,
Child I called him, smiling: but he smiled
Back, as one too high for vain annoy—
    Not a child.

II

Not a child? alack the year!
What should ail an undefiled
Heart, that he would fain appear
    Not a child?

Men, with years and memories piled
Each on other, far and near,
Fain again would so be styled:

Fain would cast off hope and fear,
Rest, forget, be reconciled:
Why would you so fain be, dear,
    Not a child?

III

Child or boy, my darling, which you will,
Still your praise finds heart and song employ,
Heart and song both yearning toward you still,
    Child or boy.

All joys else might sooner pall or cloy
Love than this which inly takes its fill,
Dear, of sight of your more perfect joy.

Nay, be aught you please, let all fulfil
All your pleasure; be your world your toy:
Mild or wild we love you, loud or still,
    Child or boy.

        —ALGERNON CHARLES SWINBURNE

From *Collected Poetical Works,* Vol. 2, by Algernon Charles Swinburne. Copyright, by Harper & Brothers.

THE BOY I LOVE

My boy, do you know the boy I love?
    I fancy I see him now;
His forehead bare in the sweet spring air,
With the wind of hope in his waving hair,
    The sunrise on his brow.

He is something near your height, may be;
    And just about your years;
Timid as you; but his will is strong,
And his love of right and his hate of wrong
    Are mightier than his fears.

He has the courage of simple truth.
    The trial that he must bear,
The peril, the ghost that frights him most,
He faces boldly, and like a ghost
    It vanishes in air.

As wildfowl take, by river and lake,
    The sunshine and the rain,
With cheerful, constant hardihood
He meets the bad luck and the good,
    The pleasure and the pain.

Come friends in need? With heart and deed
    He gives himself to them.
He has the grace which reverence lends,—
Reverence, the crowning flower that bends
    The upright lily-stem.

Though deep and strong his sense of wrong,
    Fiery his blood and young,

His spirit is gentle, his heart is great,
He is swift to pardon and slow to hate,
    And master of his tongue.

Fond of his sports? No merrier lad's
    Sweet laughter ever rang!
But he is so generous and so frank,
His wildest wit or his maddest prank
    Can never cause a pang.

His own sweet ease, all things that please,
    He loves, like any boy;
But fosters a prudent fortitude;
Nor will he squander a future good
    To buy a fleeting joy.

Face brown or fair? I little care,
    Whatever the hue may be,
Or whether his eyes are dark or light;
If his tongue be true and his honor bright,
    He is still the boy for me.

Where does he dwell? I cannot tell;
    Nor do I know his name.
Or poor, or rich? I don't mind which;
Or learning Latin, or digging ditch;
    I love him all the same.

With high, brave heart perform your part,
    Be noble and kind as he,
Then, some fair morning, when you pass,
Fresh from glad dreams, before your glass,
    His likeness you may see.

You are puzzled? What! you think there is not
    A boy like him,—surmise
That he is only a bright ideal?
But you have power to make him real,
    And clothe him to our eyes.

You have rightly guessed: in each pure breast
    Is his abiding-place.
Then let your own true life portray
His beauty, and blossom day by day
    With something of his grace.

                    —JOHN TOWNSEND TROWBRIDGE

From *Poetical Works,* by John Townsend Trowbridge. Reprinted
by permission of his son, Mr. Arthur T. Trowbridge.

*

CONCERNING A STORM

The other night before the storm,
I sat and watched the rain-clouds swarm
Like great, black bees, so angry that
They buzzed with thunder. Well, I sat
And saw the wind come racing down,
Banging the shutters of the town;
Kicking the dust up in the road
And frightening every little toad.
He broke off branches for a toy,
Just like a large and wicked boy;
He threw the papers in the air,

And laughed as if he didn't care
What any one might say or do.
He roared and sang and whistled, too . . .
Well, pretty soon things got so black
There was no sky except a crack,
One little streak of funny light.
"See," father said, "just see how bright
The heavens shine behind it now—
And look, it seemed to spread somehow."
But father didn't understand
That I had seen it—seen God's hand
When, in a flash, so sharp and sly,
He tore a hole in that black sky.
I guess God must have missed my face
Behind the clouds in that dark place,
And so He made a hole to see
Whatever had become of me.
So when the space grew red and wide
And full of gold, and father cried,
"Was ever such a brilliant hue—"
I only smiled because I knew
I had been looking in God's eye . . .
Yet I kept still, till by and by,
When father cried, "The lightning, see—"
I had to laugh out loud with glee,
For it was God that winked at me!

—LOUIS UNTERMEYER

THE TOYS

My little Son, who look'd from thoughtful eyes
And moved and spoke in quiet grown-up wise,
Having my law the seventh time disobey'd,
I struck him, and dismiss'd
With hard words and unkiss'd,
His Mother, who was patient, being dead.
Then, fearing lest his grief should hinder sleep,
I visited his bed,
But found him slumbering deep,
With darken'd eyelids, and their lashes yet
From his late sobbing wet.
And I, with moan,
Kissing away his tears, left others of my own;
For, on a table drawn beside his head,
He had put, within his reach,
A box of counters and a red-vein'd stone,
A piece of glass abraded by the beach
And six or seven shells,
A bottle with bluebells
And two French copper coins, ranged there with careful
    art,
To comfort his sad heart.
So when that night I pray'd
To God, I wept, and said:
Ah, when at last we lie with tranced breath,
Not vexing Thee in death,
And Thou rememberest of what toys
We made our joys,
How weakly understood,
Thy great commanded good,
Then, fatherly not less

Than I whom Thou hast moulded from the clay,
Thou'lt leave Thy wrath, and say,
'I will be sorry for their childishness.'

—COVENTRY PATMORE

From *Poems,* by Coventry Patmore. Copyright, 1906, by George Bell.

*

LAWYER AND CHILD

How large was Alexander, father,
    That parties designate
The historic gentleman as rather
    Inordinately great?

Why, son, to speak with conscientious
    Regard for history,
Waiving all claims, of course, to heights pretentious,—
    About the size of me.

—JAMES WHITCOMB RILEY

From *Rhymes of Childhood,* by James Whitcomb Riley. Copyright, 1890-1918. Used by special permission of the publishers, The Bobbs-Merrill Company.

*

MISFORTUNE

I found a bird's nest in a tree,
And asked my Pop to come and see
The cunning baby birds with me.

But Pop was busy, and he guessed
He didn't care to see the nest.

So, though I love him just as much,
I feel that we are not in touch
About some things I love.
And I will never bother him
To come and bend me down a limb
And see the nest above.

—RALPH BERGENGREN

*

DAD 'N' ME

I

A youngster's 'mighty lucky
If he's got a fishin' dad;
The fun I used to have with mine
Was the best I ever had,
When the sundown called the music
From the bullfrog's husky throat
And we were trollin' pick'rel
In an old, flat-bottom'd boat.

II

We always used a hand-line
With a whirlin' silver spoon,

And we both took turns at rowin'
Till the risin' summer moon
Her warnin' of the nightfall
With her silver pencil wrote,
And we'd quit trollin' pick'rel
In the old, flat-bottom'd boat.

III

In the dusk of early ev'nin'
Fish 'll strike a shinin' bait.
Droppin' softly down slow water
We would lure 'em to their fate,
Pilin' up a feast for breakfast
Worth a twenty-dollar note
By just a-trollin' pick'rel
In an old, flat-bottom'd boat.

IV

So I'm goin' back this summer
To the fun I can't forget,
And when the shadows lengthen
'Cross the old mill-pond, you bet
We'll be droppin' down the river,
Past the lily fronds we'll float—
Dad 'n' me a-trollin' pick'rel
In an old, flat-bottom'd boat.

—STUART N. LAKE

From the *Outlook*, and reprinted by permission of the author.

A FATHER'S PRAYER

God, you have given me a son:
    Now help me make him worthy of
    His father's name, his father's love;
Among companions, make him one
    Both clean of heart and clean of speech;
    Help me my son these things to teach.

God, you have given me a boy:
    Now help me still my boy to rear;
    Too kind to quarrel, brave to fear,
Too good for any sinful joy,
    Or, if temptation prove too strong,
    Too wise to follow folly long.

God, you a son have given me:
    Help me to make my boy a man,
    Help me to teach him all I can
Of honesty and decency—
    Father of fathers, make me one,
    A fit example for a son.

—DOUGLAS MALLOCH

From *Come On Home,* by Douglas Malloch. Copyrighted by the author and reprinted with his permission.

*

ALEC YEATON'S SON

Gloucester, August, 1720

The wind it wailed, the wind it moaned,
    And the white caps flecked the sea;

"An' I would to God," the skipper groaned,
"I had not my boy with me!"

Snug in the stern-sheets, little John
    Laughed as the scud swept by;
But the skipper's sunburnt cheek grew wan
    As he watched the wicked sky.

"Would he were at his mother's side!"
    And the skipper's eyes were dim.
"Good Lord in heaven, if ill betide,
    What would become of him!

"For me—my muscles are as steel,
    For me let hap what may;
I might make shift upon the keel
    Until the break o' day.

"But he, he is so weak and small,
    So young scarce learned to stand—
O pitying Father of us all,
    I trust him in Thy hand!

"For Thou, who markest from on high
    A sparrow's fall—each one!—
Surely, O Lord, thou 'lt have an eye
    On Alec Yeaton's son!"

Then, helm hard-port; right straight he sailed
    Towards the headland light:
The wind it moaned, the wind it wailed,
    And black, black fell the night.

Then burst a storm to make one quail
    Though housed from winds and waves—
They who could tell about that gale
    Must rise from watery graves!

Sudden it came, as sudden went;
    Ere half the night was sped,
The winds were hushed, the waves were spent,
    And the stars shone overhead.

Now, as the morning mist grew thin,
    The folk on Gloucester shore
Saw a little figure floating in
    Secure, on a broken oar!

Up rose the cry, "A wreck! a wreck!
    Pull, mates, and waste no breath!"—
They knew it, though 't was but a speck
    Upon the edge of death!

Long did they marvel in the town
    At God his strange decree,
That let the stalwart skipper drown
    And the little child go free!

             —THOMAS BAILEY ALDRICH

DADDY

It's good to take the dusty road
      With daddy,
To shoulder my share of a camper's load
      Like daddy;
Flee for a night all coddling care,
The dreads and the dangers of darkness share,
With the stars in my eyes and the dew in my hair—
      And daddy.

It's fun to sit by the crackling fire
      With daddy,
While the flames leap high and the sparks mount higher
      For daddy;
To break for once the home food ban—
Eat with my fingers out of a pan
And chatter along as man to man
      With daddy.

It's great to stretch on a sweet pine bed
      By daddy,
To vision the trails that lie ahead
      With daddy;
Gaze for a while at the spangled sky,
Sleepily smile to the man close by
And yield to Nature's lullaby
      With daddy.

Then the dawn—the dawn—and the dusty way
      With daddy!
Another vagabondish day
      With daddy;
No call has he, no cares annoy;

He's all my own, and mine the joy
Of finding the very heart of a boy
          In daddy.
                              —ROBERT FREEMAN

*

MY PIPE

My pipe is old
And caked with soot;
My wife remarks:
"How can you put
That horrid relic,
So unclean,
Inside your mouth?
The nicotine
Is strong enough
To stupefy
A Swedish plumber."
I reply:

"This is the kind
Of pipe I like:
I fill it full
Of Happy Strike,
Or Barking Cat
Or Cabman's Puff,
Or Brooklyn Bridge
(That potent stuff)

Or Chaste Embraces,
Knacker's Twist,
Old Honeycomb
Or Niggerfist.

I clamp my teeth
Upon its stem—
It is my bliss,
My diadem.
Whatever Fate
May do to me,
This is my favourite
 B
B B.
For this dear pipe
You feign to scorn
I smoked the night
The boy was born."

—CHRISTOPHER MORLEY

From *Songs for a Little House,* by Christopher Morley. Copyright, 1917, by Doubleday, Doran & Company, Inc.

*

WISHES FOR MY SON

Born on Saint Cecilia's Day, 1912

Now, my son, is life for you,
And I wish you joy of it—
Joy of power in all you do,
Deeper passion, better wit

Than I had who had enough,
Quicker life and length thereof,
More of every gift but love.

Love I have beyond all men,
Love that now you share with me—
What have I to wish you then
But that you be good and free,
And that God to you may give
Grace in stronger days to live?

For I wish you more than I
Ever knew of glorious deed,
Though no rapture passed me by
That an eager heart could heed,
Though I followed heights and sought
Things the sequel never brought.

Wild and perilous holy things
Flaming with a martyr's blood,
And the joy that laughs and sings
Where a foe must be withstood,
Joy of headlong happy chance
Leading on the battle dance.

But I found no enemy,
No man in a world of wrong,
That Christ's word of charity
Did not render clean and strong—
Who was I to judge my kind,
Blindest groper of the blind?

God to you may give the sight
And the clear, undoubting strength
Wars to knit for single right,

Freedom's war to knit at length,
And to win through wrath and strife,
To the sequel of my life.

But for you, so small and young,
Born on Saint Cecilia's Day,
I in more harmonious song
Now for nearer joys should pray—
Simpler joys: the natural growth
Of your childhood and your youth,
Courage, innocence and truth:

These for you, so small and young,
In your hand and heart and tongue.

—THOMAS MACDONAGH

From *Poetical Works,* by Thomas MacDonagh, and reprinted by
permission of The Talbot Press, Ltd., Dublin, Ireland.

*

LITTLE SON

The very acme of my woe,
    The pivot of my pride,
My consolation, and my hope
    Deferred, but not denied.
The substance of my every dream,
    The riddle of my plight,
The very world epitomized
    In turmoil and delight.

—GEORGIA DOUGLAS JOHNSON

Reprinted by permission of the author.

SOME YOUNGSTER'S DAD

The greatest man who ever was,
    He isn't king or president.
You never heard of him, because
    He didn't anything invent,
Or write a book, or form a trust,
    Or sing a song to make us glad,
Or win a battle—he is just
    Some youngster's dad.

You talk about your Washingtons
    And Grants and other persons great.
They may be big—but to our sons
    They're rather vague at any rate.
But Dad, their dad! He's here and now,
    The best a fellow ever had;
There's one great person anyhow—
    Some youngster's dad.

"My dad makes lots of money." "Mine
    Can knock a ball a half a mile."
"My dad can play a jews'-harp fine."
    "Mine keeps us laffin' all the while."
"My dad could lick a wildcat—gee,
    You ought to see him when he's mad!"
You have to be a man to be
    Some youngster's dad.

"My dad he used to have a horse—"
    "My dad can shoot ducks on the wing."
"My dad's the best man on the force—
    He ain't afraid of anything."
"My dad will run for Congress, too,

And beat the Democrats so bad—"
Oh, lucky fellow man, are you
    Some youngster's dad?

The man who sits upon a throne
    Or other eminence as high,
The man who far and wide is known
    And always in the public eye,
Must watch his step for fear he fall—
    But, worshipped by some little tad,
There is the greatest job of all—
    Some youngster's dad.

You may not worry much about
    Religion, which is right or wrong,
But here's a thing, without a doubt,
    To keep you straight and keep you strong,
Here's your responsibility,
    The greatest mortal ever had—
Just to be worthy, friend, to be
    Some youngster's dad.

—DOUGLAS MALLOCH

A TALK TO THE BOY

Come, boy, to your dad. Let me tell you some things
    Of the man who loved me as I'm now loving you.
For the heart is a pendulum, heavy, that swings
    Aye forward and back, as all pendulums do.

And tonight, mine has swung far away to the time
    When your dad had a dad—just as you have, my
        son;
A dad to whose arms I was welcome to climb
    When his day in the cornfield or meadow was done.

I crept into arms that were stronger, my lad;
    And his hands—O, so tender!—were harder than
        mine.
For the world had been harsh with the dad of your dad.
    Yet I wish that my soul were as gentle and fine
As the one roughly clad in that body of his
    That so lavishly gave of its strength for the one
Who now shelters you. And my prayer's burden is
    That you may think thus of your father, my son.

What I've gained, I have gained; his the heavier cost.
    He, in embryo, held all the things I have done.
Yet I fear—gravely fear there are things I have lost
    That sadly diminish the triumph, my son.
So lie close, little man; there's so little we know
    Except that I love you and you can love me.
And I smile with content that you're loving me so,
    And am glad in that love, as my dad used to be.

               —STRICKLAND GILLILAN.

From *Including You and Me,* by Strickland Gillilan. Copyright, 1916, by Forbes & Co.

KIDDUSH

Yesterday father said a prayer
    At table, over wine and bread;
He broke the loaf and sipped the wine,
    Then put his hand upon my head.

He does this every Friday night
    Just before we sit and eat.
After mother's blessed the lights
    He thanks God for our bread and meat;

Then puts his hand upon my head
    And blesses me, while mother stands
With lowered head and downcast eyes,
    And pats my arm with both her hands.

And why should they do all of this
    For just a little boy like me?
I think it's only 'cause they hope
    That a good man I'll grow to be.
              —LEAH RACHEL YOFFIE

*

PLAYMATES

Why did you grow so big, Daddy,
    With me so very small,
For don't you see how many games
    We just can't play at all?

For when we're playing circus
    And riding round the track,

I never can be elephant
With you upon my back—
And when down in the garden
You swing me very high,
I never can give you a turn,
And make you touch the sky.

If you were small, like me, Daddy,
We'd splash about together—
Close under my umbrella—in
The lovely rainy weather!
I'd let you push me in my cart
Down to the picture show,
And then I'd push you home again
As fast as I could go!

Why did you grow so big, Daddy,
    With me so very small,
For don't you see how many games
    We just can't play at all?

—MARY WHITE SLATER

From 1915, *Arbor and Bird Day Manual*. Reprinted by permission
of the State of Ohio Department of Education.

*

THE WAY HE USED TO DO

Sometimes when I come in at night
    And take my shoes off at the stair,
I hear my Pop turn on the light
    And holler: "William, are you there?"

And then he says: "You go to bed—
I knew that stealthy step was you."
And I asked how and then he said:
"'Cause that's the way I used to do."

Sometimes when I come home at six
O'clock and hurry up my chores,
And get a big armful of sticks
Of wood and bring it all indoors,
My Pop he comes and feels my head
And says: "You've been in swimmin'—you!"
When I asked how he knew, he said:
"'Cause that's the way I used to do."

Sometimes before a circus comes,
When I'm as willing as can be
To do my chores, and all my chums
They all take turns at helping me,
My Pop, he pats 'em on the head
And says: "You like a circus, too?"
When I asked how he knew, he said:
"'Cause that's the way I used to do."

And lots of times when he gets mad
Enough to whip me and declares
He never saw another lad
Like I am—well, at last he spares
Me from a whipping and he lays
His rawhide down: "I can't whip you
For that, although I should," he says,
"'Cause that's the way I used to do."

—James W. Foley

FOR AN ARGONAUT, AGE SEVEN

When you are tall and old and far too wise
 For lore of picture-book and fairy story,
You will go forth with gay audacious eyes
 To seek the savage lands of alien glory.

Singapore you may see, and Samarkand;
 Sapphire ports where swart sea-rovers rest;
On Mongol tundra or Saharan sand
 Forgotten fires will chart your lonely quest.

Yet will you ever know again a wonder
 As poignant-sweet as that your heart confesses
In trailing caravans of pirate plunder
 Across the wood-lot's shadowy wildernesses?

And though romance may halo peak and foam,
 Will all her treasures prove one tithe as rich
As those your laden argosies bring home
 Down the wide reaches of the garden ditch?

       —TED OLSON

Reprinted by permission of *Sunset Magazine,* September, 1925.

     *

GETTING INFORMATION OUT OF PA

 My pa he didn't go to town
  Last evening after tea,
 But got a book and settled down
  As comfy as could be.

I'll tell you I was offul glad
   To have my pa about
To answer all the things I had
   Been tryin' to find out.

And so I asked him why the world
   Is round instead of square,
And why the piggies' tails are curled,
   And why don't fish breathe air?
And why the moon don't hit a star,
   And why the dark is black,
And just how many birds there are,
   And will the wind come back?

And why does water stay in wells,
   And why do June bugs hum,
And what's the roar I hear in shells,
   And when will Christmas come?
And why the grass is always green,
   Instead of sometimes blue,
And why a bean will grow a bean
   And not an apple, too?

And why a horse can't learn to moo,
   And why a cow can't neigh?
And do the fairies live on dew,
   And what makes hair grow gray—
And then my pa got up an' gee!
   The offul words he said,
I hadn't done a thing, but he
   Jest sent me off to bed.

                —Anonymous.

From *One Hundred Choice Selections*. Used by permission of and arrangement with The Penn Publishing Company, Philadelphia.

THE BRIDGE BUILDER

An old man going a lone highway,
Came, at the evening cold and gray,
To a chasm vast and deep and wide.
The old man crossed in the twilight dim,
The sullen stream had no fear for him;
But he turned when safe on the other side
And built a bridge to span the tide.

"Old man," said a fellow pilgrim near,
"You are wasting your strength with building here;
Your journey will end with the ending day,
You never again will pass this way;
You've crossed the chasm, deep and wide,
Why build this bridge at evening tide?"

The builder lifted his old gray head;
"Good friend, in the path I have come," he said,
"There followed after me to-day
A youth whose feet must pass this way.
This chasm that has been as naught to me
To that fair-haired youth may a pitfall be;
He, too, must cross in the twilight dim;
Good friend, I am building this bridge for him!"

—Anonymous

*

A BOY'S TRUST

I made a sort of promise I might go
Down to the place with him sometime. I know,
We somehow live out of child-sight, and ways
Of things expected so.

He would not ask my confidence again;
And I forgot, yet wondered at the pain
That sought to tell me something with his eyes,
His lips would not explain.

His stocky leg entwined about a chair,
His brown hands fidgeting as he swung there
I tried to read his melancholy pout
That dogged me everywhere.

Something it was he had expected me
To share alone with him, to go and see;
I knew the trust—a child's part of myself,
Mine, of the man-to-be.

—LEO C. TURNER

Reprinted from *Poetry, A Magazine of Verse,* and with the permission of the author.

*

ANECDOTE FOR FATHERS

I have a boy of five years old;
His face is fair and fresh to see;
His limbs are cast in beauty's mould,
And dearly he loves me.

One morn we strolled on our dry walk,
Our quiet home all full in view,
And held such intermitted talk
As we are wont to do.

My thoughts on former pleasures ran;
I thought of Kilve's delightful shore,
Our pleasant home when spring began,
A long, long year before.

A day it was when I could bear
Some fond regrets to entertain;
With so much happiness to spare,
I could not feel a pain.

The green earth echoed to the feet
Of lambs that bounded through the glade,
From shade to sunshine, and as fleet
From sunshine back to shade.

Birds warbled round me—and each trace
Of inward sadness had its charm;
Kilve, thought I, was a favoured place,
And so is Liswyn farm.

My boy beside me tripped, so slim
And graceful in his rustic dress!
And, as we talked, I questioned him,
In very idleness.

'Now tell me, had you rather be,'
I said, and took him by the arm,
'On Kilve's smooth shore, by the green sea,
Or here at Liswyn farm?'

In careless mood he looked at me,
While still I held him by the arm,
And said, 'At Kilve I'd rather be
Than here at Liswyn farm.'

'Now, little Edward, say why so:
My little Edward, tell me why.'—
'I cannot tell, I do not know.'—
'Why, this is strange,' said I;

'For, here are woods, hills smooth and warm:
There surely must some reason be
Why you would change sweet Liswyn farm
For Kilve by the green sea.'

At this, my boy hung down his head,
He blushed with shame, nor made reply;
And three times to the child I said,
'Why, Edward, tell me why?'

His head he raised—there was in sight,
It caught his eye, he saw it plain—
Upon the house-top, glittering bright,
A broad and gilded vane.

Then did the boy his tongue unlock,
And eased his mind with this reply:
'At Kilve there was no weather-cock;
And that's the reason why.'

O dearest, dearest boy! my heart
For better lore would seldom yearn,
Could I but teach the hundredth part
Of what from thee I learn.

—WILLIAM WORDSWORTH

From *Childhood in Verse and Prose,* edited by S. Miles. Copyright, 1923, by Oxford University Press.

MY SON

I that had yearned for youth, my own, again,
    And mourned the wasted hours of younger days,
I that had sighed for Spring, for Summer, when
    The snows of Winter covered all my ways—
I that had prayed for years, for only one,
    Have found that prayer answered in my son.

He is myself again, with hopes of old,
    With old temptations and with old desires;
He is myself again—the clay to mold
    Into the man, and all the man aspires.
Who says that youth returns to us no more?
    He is as I was in the days of yore.

In my own days, in my own days of youth,
    Ah, how I wished a comrade and a friend!—
To help me keep the quiet path of truth
    And through temptation my own feet attend.
So shall I journey onward by his side,
    His father—yea, his comrade and his guide.

I that have failed shall shape success in him,
    I that have wandered point the proper path,
I signal when the signal lights are dim,
    A roof to fend him from the storms of wrath—
So we shall 'journey upward, I and he,
    And he shall be the man I meant to be.

                              —Douglas Malloch

From *Heart Content*, by Douglas Malloch. Copyrighted by the
author and reprinted with his permission.

OUR WHIPPINGS

Come, Harvey, let us sit awhile and talk about the times
Before you went to selling clothes and I to peddling
    rhymes—
The days when we were little boys, as naughty little boys
As ever worried home-folks with their everlasting noise!
Egad! and, were we so disposed, I'll venture we could
    show
The scars of wallopings we got some forty years ago;
What wallopings I mean I think I need not specify—
Mother's whippings didn't hurt, but father's! oh, my!

The way that we played hookey those many years ago—
We'd rather give 'most anything than have our children
    know!
The thousand naughty things we did, the thousand fibs
    we told—
Why, thinking of them makes my Presbyterian blood
    run cold!
How often Deacon Sabine Morse remarked if we were
    his
He'd tan our "pesky little hides until the blisters riz!"
It's many a hearty thrashing to that Deacon Morse we
    owe—
Mother's whippings didn't count—father's did, though!

We used to sneak off swimmin' in those careless, boyish
    days,
And come back home of evenings with our necks and
    backs ablaze;
How mother used to wonder why our clothes were full
    of sand,
But father, having been a boy, appeared to understand.

And, after tea, he'd beckon us to join him in the shed
Where he'd proceed to tinge our backs a deeper, darker
     red;
Say what we will of mother's, there is none will controvert
The proposition that our father's lickings always hurt!

For mother was by nature so forgiving and so mild
That she inclined to spare the rod although she spoiled the
     child;
And when at last in self-defense she had to whip us, she
Appeared to feel those whippings a great deal more than
     we!
But how we bellowed and took on, as if we'd like to die—
Poor mother really thought she hurt, and that's what
     made *her* cry!
Then how we youngsters snickered as out the door we
     slid,
For mother's whippings never hurt, though father's
     always did.

In after years poor father simmered down to five feet
     four,
But in our youth he seemed to us in height eight feet
     or more!
Oh, how we shivered when he quoth in cold, suggestive
     tone:
"I'll see you in the woodshed after supper all alone!"
Oh, how the legs and arms and dust and trouser buttons
     flew—
What florid vocalisms marked that vesper interview!
Yes, after all this lapse of years, I feelingly assert,
With all respect to mother, it was father's whippings hurt.

The little boy experiencing that tinglin' neath his vest
Is often loath to realize that all is for the best;

Yet, when the boy gets older, he pictures with delight
The buffetings of childhood—as we do here to-night.
The years, the gracious years, have smoothed and beauti-
    fied the ways
That to our little feet seemed all too rugged in the days
Before you went to selling clothes and I to peddling
    rhymes—
So, Harvey, let us sit awhile and think upon those times.

—Eugene Field

From *Poems,* by Eugene Field. Copyright, 1926, by Charles Scrib-
ner's Sons, and reprinted by their permission.

*

FATHERHOOD

My baby boy, I sing of thee
    Because thou art like song to me.
Thy joys and fears, thy smiles and tears,
    Are rhythmic in their rising;
Thy pantomimes, like tropes and rhymes,
    Are full of sweet surprising.
        A little lyric bit thou art;
        A drama quickens in thy heart,
            Concealed forsooth;
            But through thy deep soul-magic
            I see the truth,—
            Thy comedies are tragic.

Thou atom of the ages,
    Thou force among the forces
    Out from the Source of sources,
Thou puzzler of the sages,

Back comes to me thy mimicry;
This heart of mine beats on in thine,
One life Divine—
Thy destiny
In me.

—PATTERSON DuBois

*

TO A USURPER

Aha! a traitor in the camp,
A rebel strangely bold,—
A lisping, laughing, toddling scamp,
Not more than four years old!

To think that I, who've ruled alone
So proudly in the past,
Should be ejected from my throne
By my own son at last!

He trots his treason to and fro,
As only babies can,
And says he'll be his mamma's beau
When he's a "gweat, big man"!

You stingy boy! you've always had
A share in mamma's heart.
Would you begrudge your poor old dad
The tiniest little part?

That mamma, I regret to see,
  Inclines to take your part,—
As if a dual monarchy
  Should rule her gentle heart!

But when the years of youth have sped,
  The bearded man, I trow,
Will quite forget he ever said
  He'd be his mamma's beau.

Renounce your treason, little son,
  Leave mamma's heart to me;
For there will come another one
  To claim your loyalty.

And when that other comes to you,
  God grant her love may shine,
Through all your life, as fair and true
  As mamma's does through mine!

—EUGENE FIELD

From *Poems,* by Eugene Field. Copyright, 1926, by Charles
Scribner's Sons, and reprinted by their permission.

*

MAKING A MAN

When you've something hard to do,
  Laddie dear, don't shirk;
But pitch right in with all your might,
  And work, and work, and work.

'Twill never help to sit and sigh,
  So hurry and begin;

And first you know, my little lad,
    You'll find you're going to win.

When you've something hard to do,
    Remember this, my boy:
These dreaded tasks that come your way
    Will bring you pride and joy.

For if you do each duty
    Just the very best you can,
Then every time you win
    Will make you that much more a man.

          —CAROLYN R. FREEMAN

From *Bright Ideas for Easter, Mother's Day, and Children's Day,*
by Carolyn R. Freeman and others. Copyright, 1926, by The Willis
N. Bugbee Co., Syracuse, N. Y.

*

MY SERIOUS SON

My serious son! I see thee look
First on the picture, then the book.
I catch the wish that thou couldst paint
The yearnings of the ecstatic saint.
Give it not up, my serious son!
Wish it again, and it is done.
Seldom will any fail who tries
With patient hand and stedfast eyes,
And wooes the true with such pure sighs.

          —WALTER SAVAGE LANDOR

From *Book of English Verse on Infancy and Childhood,* compiled
by L. S. Wood. Copyright, 1921. By permission of The Macmillan
Company, publishers.

THE CHILD'S HERITAGE

O, there are those, a sordid clan,
With pride in gaud and faith in gold,
Who prize the sacred soul of man
For what his hands have sold.

And these shall deem thee humbly bred:
They shall not hear, they shall not see
The kings among the lordly dead
Who walk and talk with thee!

A tattered cloak may be thy dole
And thine the roof that Jesus had:
The broidered garment of the soul
Shall keep thee purple-clad!

The blood of men hath dyed its brede,
And it was wrought by holy seers
With sombre dream and golden deed
And pearled with women's tears.

With Eld thy chain of days is one:
The seas are still Homeric seas;
Thy sky shall glow with Pindar's sun,
The stars of Socrates!

Unaged the ancient tide shall surge,
The old Spring burn along the bough:
The new and old for thee converge
In one eternal Now!

I give thy feet the hopeful sod,
Thy mouth, the priceless boon of breath;

The glory of the search for God
Be thine in life and death!

Unto thy flesh, the soothing dust;
Thy soul, the gift of being free:
The torch my fathers gave in trust,
Thy father gives to thee!

—JOHN G. NEIHARDT

*

THE LITTLE BOY LOST

"Father, father, where are you going?
    O do not walk so fast.
Speak, father, speak to your little boy,
    Or else I shall be lost."

The night was dark, no father was there,
    The child was wet with dew;
The mire was deep, and the child did weep,
    And away the vapour flew.

—WILLIAM BLAKE

*

HIS CHRISTMAS SLED

He winks at twinklings of the frost,
    And on his airy race,
Its tingles beat to redder heat
    The rapture of his face:—

The colder, keener is the air,
    The less he cares a feather.
But, there! he's gone! and I gaze on
    The wintriest of weather!

Ah, Boy! still speeding o'er the track
    Where none returns again,
To sigh for you, or cry for you,
    Or die for you were vain.—
And so, speed on! the while I pray
    All nipping frosts forsake you—
Ride still ahead of grief, but may
    All glad things overtake you!

—JAMES WHITCOMB RILEY

From *Rhymes of Childhood,* by James Whitcomb Riley. Copyright, 1890-1918. Used by special permission of the publishers, The Bobbs-Merrill Company.

*

MY BOY

You smile and you smoke your cigar, my boy;
    You walk with a languid swing;
You tinkle and tune your guitar, my boy,
    And lift up your voice and sing;
The midnight moon is a friend of yours,
    And a serenade your joy—
And it's only an age like mine that cures
    A trouble like yours, my boy!

—JAMES WHITCOMB RILEY

From The Biographical Edition of *The Complete Works of James Whitcomb Riley.* Copyright, 1913. Used by special permission of the publishers, The Bobbs-Merrill Company.

OPPORTUNITY

With doubt and dismay you are smitten,
　　You think there's no chance for you, son?
Why, the best books haven't been written,
　　The best race hasn't been run,
The best score hasn't been made yet,
　　The best song hasn't been sung,
The best tune hasn't been played yet,
　　Cheer up, for the world is young!

No chance? Why, the world is just eager
　　For things that you ought to create;
Its store of true wealth is still meager,
　　Its needs are incessant and great,
It yearns for more power and beauty,
　　More laughter and love and romance,
More loyalty, labor and duty,
　　No chance—why, there's nothing but chance!

For the best verse hasn't been rhymed yet,
　　The best house hasn't been planned,
The highest peak hasn't been climbed yet,
　　The mightiest rivers aren't spanned.
Don't worry and fret, faint-hearted,
　　The chances have just begun,
For the best jobs haven't been started,
　　The best work hasn't been done.

　　　　　　　　—BERTON BRALEY

BOY AND FATHER

The boy Alexander understands his father to be a famous
 lawyer.
The leather law books of Alexander's father fill a room
 like hay in a barn.
Alexander has asked his father to let him build a house
 like bricklayers build, a house with walls and roofs
 made of big leather law books.

  The rain beats on the windows
  And the raindrops run down the window glass
  And the raindrops slide off the green blinds down the
   siding.

The boy Alexander dreams of Napoleon in John C.
 Abbott's history, Napoleon the grand and lonely man
 wronged, Napoleon in his life wronged and in his
 memory wronged.
The boy Alexander dreams of the cat Alice saw, the cat
 fading off into the dark and leaving the teeth of its
 Cheshire smile lighting the gloom.

Buffaloes, blizzards, way down in Texas, in the panhandle
 of Texas snuggling close to New Mexico,
These creep into Alexander's dreaming by the window
 when his father talks with strange men about land
 down in Deaf Smith County.
Alexander's father tells the strange men: Five years ago
 we ran a Ford out on the prairie and chased
 antelopes.

Only once or twice in a long while has Alexander heard
 his father say 'my first wife' so-and-so and such-
 and-such.

A few times softly the father has told Alexander, 'Your
    mother . . . was a beautiful woman . . . but we
    won't talk about her.'
Always Alexander listens with a keen listen when he hears
    his father mention 'my first wife' or 'Alexander's
    mother.'

Alexander's father smokes a cigar and the Episcopal
    rector smokes a cigar, and the words come often:
    mystery of life, mystery of life.
These two come into Alexander's head blurry and grey
    while the rain beats on the windows and the rain-
    drops run down the window glass and the raindrops
    slide off the green blinds and down the siding.
These and: There is a God, there must be a God, how
    can there be rain or sun unless there is a God?

So from the wrongs of Napoleon and the Cheshire cat
    smile on to the buffaloes and blizzards of Texas and
    on to his mother and to God, so the blurry grey rain
    dreams of Alexander have gone on five minutes,
    maybe ten, keeping slow easy time to the raindrops
    on the window glass and the raindrops sliding off
    the green blinds and down the siding.

—Carl Sandburg

*

TO VINCENT CORBET, HIS SON

What I shall leave thee, none can tell,
But all shall say I wish thee well:

I wish thee, Vin, before all wealth,
Both bodily and ghostly health;
Nor too much wealth nor wit come to thee,
So much of either may undo thee.
I wish thee learning not for show,
Enough for to instruct and know;
Not such as gentlemen require
To prate at table or at fire.
I wish thee all thy mother's graces,
Thy father's fortunes and his places.
I wish thee friends, and one at court,
Not to build on, but support;
To keep thee not in doing many
Oppressions, but from suffering any.
I wish thee peace in all thy ways,
Nor lazy nor contentious days;
And, when thy soul and body part,
As innocent as now thou art.

—RICHARD CORBET

From *Book of English Verse on Infancy and Childhood,* compiled by L. S. Wood. Copyright, 1921. By permission of The Macmillan Company, publishers.

*

MOTHER TO SON

Well, son, I'll tell you:
Life for me ain't been no crystal stair.
It's had tacks in it,
And splinters,
And boards torn up,

And places with no carpet on the floor—
Bare.
But all the time
I'se been a-climbin' on,
And reachin' landin's,
And turnin' corners,
And sometimes goin' in the dark
Where there ain't been no light.
So boy, don't you turn back.
Don't you set down on the steps
'Cause you finds it's kinder hard.
Don't you fall now—
For I's still goin', honey,
I'se still climbin',
And life for me ain't been no crystal stair.

—LANGSTON HUGHES

From *Weary Blues,* by Langston Hughes. By permission of and
special arrangement with Alfred A. Knopf, Inc., authorized pub-
lishers.

TO MY LITTLE SON

In your face I sometimes see
Shadowings of the man to be,
And eager, dream of what my son
Will be in twenty years and one.

But when you are to manhood grown,
And all your manhood ways are known,
Then shall I, wistful, try to trace
The child you once were in your face?

—JULIA JOHNSON DAVIS

Reprinted by permission of the author and of *The Lyric.*

IF—

If you can keep your head when all about you
 Are losing theirs and blaming it on you,
If you can trust yourself when all men doubt you,
 But make allowance for their doubting too;
If you can wait and not be tired by waiting,
 Or being lied about, don't deal in lies,
Or being hated don't give way to hating,
 And yet don't look too good, nor talk too wise:

If you can dream—and not make dreams your master;
 If you can think—and not make thoughts your aim,
If you can meet with Triumph and Disaster
 And treat those two impostors just the same;
If you can bear to hear the truth you've spoken
 Twisted by knaves to make a trap for fools,
Or watch the things you gave your life to, broken,
 And stoop and build 'em up with worn-out tools:

If you can make one heap of all your winnings
 And risk it on one turn of pitch-and-toss,
And lose, and start again at your beginnings
 And never breathe a word about your loss;
If you can force your heart and nerve and sinew
 To serve your turn long after they are gone,
And so hold on when there is nothing in you
 Except the Will which says to them: "Hold on!"

If you can talk with crowds and keep your virtue,
 Or walk with Kings—nor lose the common touch,
If neither foes nor loving friends can hurt you,
 If all men count with you, but none too much;

If you can fill the unforgiving minute
   With sixty seconds' worth of distance run,
Yours is the Earth and everything that's in it,
   And—which is more—you'll be a Man, my son!
               —RUDYARD KIPLING

*

TO MY SON

"To follow the dream—and again to follow the dream—
   and so—*ewig—usque ad finem!*"
               —CONRAD'S *"Lord Jim"*

Must you frown so?
Must you scowl so bitterly?
Oh, I know
It's very strange, after the warm, dark silence—
This cold, confused inanity.
But don't frown.
Nothing lasts forever, be assured.
Only a few years, after all, to be endured;
Then you may go back down   .
Into the tranquil nothingness.
You have my word.

What can you have heard
While you were where you were?
Did some subtle rumor seep
Into your deep

Calm of nonentity?
Can it be
They have warned you what you may expect?
Did they say how you must grope
With only a hint of what you are groping for?
And fight, and ache, and hope
And only guess what you are hoping for?
Did they say how you will see
Beauty scorned and trampled, and the ugly
Triumph of efficient swine, guzzling smugly?

Oh, it's all true enough.
You will observe
Senseless tragedy, incomprehensible pain.
And you will find you cannot do enough,
Try as you may,
To keep your white integrity
From the world's stain.
And there will be many a tortured night
When you will stare and stare,
And tear
At your own flesh, and toss, and bite
The pillow in your agony,
Because you cannot make your dream come right
(Do not delude yourself, dear boy;
One does not ever make the dream come right.)

But the dream—follow it!
Never abandon it, though the pursuing take you
Into the mire, into the desert places
Where no help is; into the filth and squalor
Clotted with brutish, empty faces;
Into destruction, death.
Not for a moment will you see it clear,

Your dream.
You must not hope to. It is the chase that matters.

Though your flesh become ribbons,
And your spirit, tatters.
Drive! Drive!
Follow the dim gleam
Follow!

There will be those who will seek to divert
Your eyes from your dream.
Many will plot and scheme
How they may blind you,
How they may bind you.
And there will be a few
Loving you,
Who will endeavor to guard you from all hurt.

Listen to none!
Yourself, you must fight through!
Defiance to the foe, gentleness to the friend,
But in the end
The way of the dream is the lonely way.
They are they.
You are you.
And what can I promise for a reward?
Is there, then, nothing but the hard
March toward
A will-o'-the-wisp,
With oblivion beyond?

Oh, yes! Along the road that you must go
You will find bits of dream-trail here and there.
Sunsets, and purple dawns, and the slow
Drift of the moon . . . melodies, and

The soft richnesses of women's hair. . . .
And lips that cling and tremble . . . or a hand
Clasping yours firmly, stanchly, joyously . . .
And there are fragrant souls that hide away,
But may be glimpsed by one who seeks . . .
Other dream-hunters, too . . .
And the compelling blue
Of the sea . . . and something that speaks
Out of the earth, in April . . . and the glow
Of ripened fruits, in autumn . . . and the sparkle
Of starlight on the snow . . . and the crisp patterns
The words can make . . . and the sweet curves
Of thighs and breasts . . . and the inscrutable fog . . .
The gay, devoted banter of a dog . . .
The bursting green of the grass, after
The pelt of rain . . . and the brooks' laughter . . .

But—enough.
Search out your own dream-stuff.
It will guide your stumbling soul
Toward the mist-enshrouded goal.

Come, now.
Set out upon your futile quest.
Chase your dream, the while you know
You will never grasp it.
Up, then! Go!
Earn your timeless rest . . .

Must you frown so? . . .

—JOHN V. A. WEAVER

THE FATHER

Hearing his son and daughter
Laugh, and talk of dances, theaters,
Of their school, and friends,
And books,
Taking it all for granted,—
He sighs a bit,
Remembering wistfully
A certain mill-town
And his boyhood there,
And puts his arm
Across his son's broad shoulder,
Dumbly, as fathers do.

—JOHN HOLMES

Reprinted by permission of the author.

*

MY FATHER'S CHAIR

(Parliaments of Henry III, 1265)

There are four good legs to my Father's Chair—
Priest and People and Lords and Crown.
I sits on all of 'em fair and square,
And that is the reason it don't break down.

I won't trust one leg, nor two, nor three,
To carry my weight when I sets me down.
I wants all four of 'em under me—
Priest and People and Lords and Crown.

I sits on all four and I favours none—
Priest, nor People, nor Lords, nor Crown—
And I never tilts in my chair, my son,
And that is the reason it don't break down!

When your time comes to sit in my Chair,
Remember your Father's habits and rules.
Sit on all four legs, fair and square,
And never be tempted by one-legged stools!

—RUDYARD KIPLING

*

POLONIUS' ADVICE TO LAERTES

Look thou character. Give thy thoughts no tongue,
Nor any unproportion'd thought his act.
Be thou familiar, but by no means vulgar:
The friends thou hast, and their adoption tried,
Grapple them to thy soul with hoops of steel;
But do not dull thy palm with entertainment
Of each new-hatch'd, unfledg'd comrade. Beware
Of entrance to a quarrel; but, being in,
Bear't that th' opposed may beware of thee.
Give every man thine ear, but few thy voice:
Take each man's censure, but reserve thy judgment.
Costly thy habit as thy purse can buy,
But not express'd in fancy; rich, not gaudy:
For the apparel oft proclaims the man.

Neither a borrower nor a lender be;
For loan oft loses both itself and friend,
And borrowing dulls the edge of husbandry.
This above all: to thine own self be true,
And it must follow, as the night the day,
Thou canst not then be false to any man.

From *Hamlet,*—WILLIAM SHAKESPEARE

*

YOUNG AND OLD

When all the world is young, lad,
    And all the trees are green;
And every goose a swan, lad,
    And every lass a queen;
Then hey for boot and horse, lad,
    And round the world away;
Young blood must have its course, lad,
    And every dog his day.

When all the world is old, lad,
    And all the trees are brown;
And all the sport is stale, lad,
    And all the wheels run down;
Creep home, and take your place there,
    The spent and maimed among;
God grant you find one face there,
    You loved when all was young.

—CHARLES KINGSLEY

From *Poems,* by Charles Kingsley. Copyright, 1902. By permission
of The Macmillan Company, publishers.

FROM MY FATHER

(For my vow-day)

Take my wish and all its meaning,
To my boy this blessed day,
Fondly tell him hearts are beating,
Greeting him though far away;
Hearts that keep their old affection,
Here beneath the loved rooftree,
Now o'erflow with joyous prayers,
For the vows this morn to be.

Greet him for me, as I've often,
Hand in hand and cheek to cheek,
Bide a few unworded moments,
Till the ready tongue can speak;
Give him them with all its fulness,—
In my inmost heart 'tis born—
"Here's a father's love, God bless it,
To my child this holy morn."

You may tell him, tho' he knows it,
That we miss the days of yore,
And the simple joys that blessed them,
How we tell them o'er and o'er!
And the fragrant fields and woodlands
Oft we walk, as when of old,
With our hands locked fast together,
Up and down their ways we strolled.

Sure you'll tell him, since he left me,
All his books are safe away,
And his trinkets o'er the mantle,
Join the fireside's merry play;

And you'll whisper that his mother,
(Half her prayers she gives to him)
To the window brings a picture,
Ere the sunset lights are dim.

Never breadth of time or distance,
Schoolboy fame or honored lore,
Weakened in his heart our memory,
Changed the smile of old he wore;
For his letters took me with him,
Over seas to far-off climes,
And from mighty books he taught me
Speech of sage and poet's rhymes.

Now he tells me of the Blackrobes,
Worldwide in unfearing strife,
Bringing through their tireless battles,
Saving Christ-rule into life;
See glad tears have marked his letter,
Where he points that morn to me,
When in vestments by the Altar
Priest of Christ he prays to be.

Oh, the passing years, how fleeting!
Oh, the waited years, how long!
And these gray hairs fear the future,
But my trust in God is strong;
Hope makes young, and faith is hopeful,
Grant, good Lord, these eyes may see
That this vow-day is foretelling—
That first Mass-morn's ecstasy.

—MICHAEL EARLS, S. J.

FATHERS AND SONS

Child to whom my loneliness
Cries—and cries, I know, in vain,—
Down the years I look and bless;
Down the years let my hand press
Strong your shoulder. I am fain
You should reap from my sown pain
Flowers of joy and loveliness,
Child I love, and love in vain.

You will never turn to me
As I turn and cry to you.
Regions strange and visions new
Shall be yours to search and see.
Old and alien I shall be.
I who love you set you free.
Yet recall I cried to you,
Child I love so utterly.

—ARTHUR DAVISON FICKE

From *The Man on the Hilltop and Other Poems,* by Arthur
Davison Ficke. Copyright, 1915, by Mitchell Kennerley, and re-
printed by permission of the author and the publisher.

*

LAMENT OF A MAN FOR HIS SON

Son, my son!

I will go up to the mountain
And there I will light a fire
To the feet of my son's spirit,

And there will I lament him;
Saying,
O my son,
What is my life to me, now you are departed!

Son, my son,
In the deep earth
We softly laid thee in a Chief's robe,
In a warrior's gear.
Surely there,
In the spirit land
Thy deeds attend thee!
Surely,
The corn comes to the ear again!

But I, here,
I am the stalk that the seed-gatherers
Descrying empty, afar, left standing.
Son, my son!
What is my life to me, now you are departed?

—MARY AUSTIN

TO A CHILD

You fly the black flag,
Pirate!
Every lift of the billow is a shift of the scales
Weighing your treasure.

No ship is safe from you, no sea.
Phoenician, Viking, common merchantman—
At last you will have them all,
Their burdens stowed in your hold,
Their gold
In which to wash your hands of duller things.
The wings of the sea-plane have already sung in your
      ears.
I have watched you, listening,
Pirate—
Child.

Yours are the wild years, the young years:
Rough weather hazards, sweet and salt of strife.
Yet they are mine, too,
These years.
They will be a flock of wild geese
Come to be fed from my hands.
I hear them, "honk, honk,"
I hear them coming
Over the grey marshes of my life.

But how can I tell you
What it will be like
When the light is behind you,
When you are old,
When the mountains have become hillocks,
And even the well of tears has dried up,
And I shall not be there to wait with you
For death?

                      —BABETTE DEUTSCH

From *Honey Out of the Rock,* by Babette Deutsch. Copyright, 1925, by D. Appleton & Company, and reprinted by their permission.

AGAINST THE WALL

If I live till my fighting days are done
I must fasten my armour on my eldest son.

I would give him better, but this is my best.
I can get along without it—I'll be glad to have a rest.

And I'll sit mending armour with my back against the
    wall,
Because I have a second son, if this one should fall.

So I'll make it very shiny and I'll whistle very loud,
And I'll clap him on the shoulder and I'll say, very proud:

 "This is the lance I used to bear!"
        But I mustn't tell what happened when I bore it.
"This is the helmet I used to wear!"
        But I won't say what befell me when I wore it.

For you couldn't tell a youngster, it wouldn't be right,
That you wish you had died in your very first fight.

And I mustn't say that victory is never worth the cost,
That defeat may be bitter, but it's better to have lost.

And I mustn't say that glory is as barren as a stone.
I'd better not say anything, but leave the lad alone.

So he'll fight very bravely and probably he'll fall:
And I'll sit mending armour with my back against the
    wall.

                              —ALINE KILMER

MARTIN LUTHER TO HIS SON, HANS

The Wonderful Garden

Grace and peace in Christ to my heartily dear little son. I see gladly that thou learnest well and prayest earnestly. Do thus, my little son, and go on. When I come home I will bring thee a fairing. (A present from the Fair.)

I know a pleasant garden wherein many children walk about. They have little golden coats, and pick up beautiful apples under the trees, and pears, cherries, and plums. They dance and are merry, and have also beautiful little ponies, with golden reins and silver saddles. Then I asked the man whose the garden is, whose children those were; he said, "These are the children who love to pray, who learn their lessons, and are good." Then I said, "Dear man, I also have a little son; he is called Hansichen Luther. Might not he also come into the garden, that he might eat such apples and pears, and ride on such beautiful little ponies, and play with these children?" Then the man said, "If he loves to pray, learns his lessons, and is good, he also shall come into the garden; Lippus and Jost also (sons of Melanchthon, friend of Luther); and when they all come together they also shall have pipes, drums, lutes, and all kinds of music; and shall dance, and shoot with little bows and arrows."

And he showed me there a fair meadow in the garden prepared for dancing. There were many pipes of pure gold, drums, and silver bows and arrows. But it was still early in the day, so that the children had not had their breakfast. Therefore I could not wait for the dancing, and said to the man, "Ah, dear sir, I will go away at once and write all this to my little son Hansichen, that he may be sure to pray and learn well and be good, so that he also may come into the garden. But he has a dear Aunt Lena; he must bring her with him." "Then," said the man, "let it be so; go and write him thus."

Therefore, my dear little son Hansichen, learn thy lessons, and pray with a cheerful heart; and tell this to Lippus and Justus, too, that they also may learn their lessons and pray. So shall you all come together into this garden. Herewith I commend you to Almighty God; and greet Aunt Lena, and give her a kiss for me.

Thy dear father,
MARTIN LUTHER

From *Fifty Famous Letters of History,* compiled by Curtis Gentry. Copyright, 1930, by the Thomas Y. Crowell Company, and used by their permission.

III

FATHERS AND DAUGHTERS

.

TO THE LITTLEST OF ALL

Little songs are prettiest,
Little tales are wittiest;
   The little, little, little cloud
     Is whitest in the west;
Little brooks are tunefullest,
Little lakes are moonfullest;
   The little, little, little trail
     Can climb the mountain best.

Little rooms are coziest,
Little hands are rosiest;
   The little, little, little home
     Is Heaven's dearer part.
Little wiles can charm a man,
Little smiles disarm a man;
   A little, little, little maid
     Can nestle in his heart.

—ARTHUR GUITERMAN

From *Mirthful Lyre,* by Arthur Guiterman. Copyright, 1918, by Harper & Brothers.

DESIGN

The curving shore was made to hold the sea,
The hollyhock to hold the drowsy bee,
The columbine to hold a drop of dew,
And my two arms were fashioned just for you.

—ARTHUR GUITERMAN

From *Mirthful Lyre,* by Arthur Guiterman. Copyright, 1918, by Harper & Brothers.

THE VANISHED FAY

Tell me, whither do they go,
All the Little Ones we know?
They "grow up" before our eyes,
And the fairy spirit flies.
Time the Piper, pied and gay—
Does he lure them all away?
Do they follow after him,
Over the horizon's brim?

Daughter's growing fair to see,
Slim and straight as popple tree;
Still a child in heart and head,
But—the fairy spirit's fled.
As a fay at break of day,
Little One has flown away,
On the stroke of fairy bell—
When and whither, who can tell?

Still her childish fancies weave
In the Land of Make Believe;
And her love of magic lore
Is as avid as before.

Dollies big and dollies small
Still are at her beck and call.
But for all this pleasant play,
Little One has gone away.

Whither, whither have they flown,
All the fays we all have known?
To what "faery lands forlorn"
On the sound of elfin horn?
As she were a woodland sprite,
Little One has vanished quite.
Waves the wand of Oberon:
Cock has crowed—the fay is gone!

—BERT LESTON TAYLOR

From *Motley Measures*, by Bert Leston Taylor. By permission of
and special arrangement with Alfred A. Knopf, Inc., authorized
publishers.

*

LOVE AT FIRST SIGHT

Not long ago I fell in love,
    But unreturned is my affection—
The girl that I'm enamored of
    Pays little heed in my direction.

I thought I knew her fairly well:
    In fact, I'd had my arm around her;
And so it's hard to have to tell
    How unresponsive I have found her.
For, though she is not frankly rude,
    Her manners quite the wrong way rub me:

It seems to me ingratitude
    To let me love her—and then snub me!

Though I'm considerate and fond,
    She shows no gladness when she spies me—
She gazes off somewhere beyond
    And doesn't even recognize me.

Her eyes, so candid, calm and blue,
    Seem asking if I can support her
In the style appropriate to
    A lady like her father's daughter.

Well, if I can't, then no one can—
    And let me add that I intend to:
She'll never know another man
    So fit for her to be a friend to.

Not love me, eh? She better had!
    By Jove, I'll make her love me one day;
For, don't you see, I am her Dad,
    And she'll be three weeks old on Sunday!
                 —CHRISTOPHER MORLEY

"AS BUSY AS I TAN BE"

A dear little lady, three summers old,
With eyes of azure, and ringlets of gold,
Is earnestly playing not far from me;
And she is as busy as she can be.

I ask her to bring me a paper or book,
When she turns toward me with a comical look
And answers, "Please, Papa, don't bozzer me,
For I is as busy as I tan be."

Yes, she is as busy as any one;
And it seems that her work is never done,
For as soon as she rises,—with eager delight,
Her labors go on without ceasing, till night.
But what if her business is mostly fun,
It's exceedingly " 'portant" and must be done;
Yet she often finds time to run errands for me,
Although she is busy as she "tan be."

She plays with her dollies, she romps with her pets,
She builds her block houses, her "lesson" she gets;
She sews for her mamma, she sweeps with her broom,
She "dusts off" her playthings, she "rights up" the room;
A thousand small things must be " 'tended to,"
All very important,—SHE only can do;
She scarcely can find time to sleep, you see,
For she is as busy as she "tan be."

A lesson we learn from this little one,
That things which are useful, will never be DONE;
And yet WE should ever be busy as she,
For there's always employment for you and me.
If this little lady finds so much to do;
There should be no idling by big folks like you;
And when she is older by many times three,
May she still keep as busy as she can be.

                              —A. B. CARROLL

WAITING FOR FATHER

In the gray of the twilight and glow of the fire,
    A little girl sat on the rug.
She was warming a slipper; and Pussy sat nigh her
    And also her friend, Mr. Pug.
And the song in the heart of the glad little girl,
As the light of the fire played over each curl,
    Was, "Father is coming—hurrah! hurrah!
    Father is coming—hurrah!"

She had spread out his soft woolen gown on the chair,
    With its facings of beautiful blue;
Had picked up her playthings that lay here and there,
    And arranged things as well as she knew.
"For the room must be tidy and pretty and bright,"
She said to herself, "when he comes, every night,
    And soon he is coming—hurrah! hurrah!
    Father is coming—hurrah!"

How rosy her cheeks, and how sparkling her eyes!
    How dimpled her soft little hand!
While Pussy and Pug look as solemn and wise
    As if the whole scene they had planned.
But you never would think, so demure are the three,
That the little maid's heart could be singing with glee:
    "Father is coming—hurrah! hurrah!
    Father is coming—hurrah!"

The sunlight has vanished, and bleak is the street,
    And beggars are dreading the night.
The pavement is noisy with home-speeding feet,
    And only the windows are bright;
When quickly the little maid springs from the rug,

Leaving Pussy half sleeping, but followed by Pug;
   "Father is coming—hurrah! hurrah!
   Father is coming—hurrah!"

                   —MARY MAPES DODGE

From *Rhymes and Jingles,* by Mary Mapes Dodge. Copyright, 1927,
by Charles Scribner's Sons.

*

FOR ALL FATHERS

Once I gave away my heart
   For a robe of fire.
Once I gave my heart to learn
   Even flames can tire.

Once my heart returned to me
   Black and bitter burned.
Seeking for a shadowed place,
   Once my heart returned.

Twice I gave away my heart
   For a lonely lack . . .
For a hollow happiness,
   So my heart came back.

Last I gave away my heart
   For a tenderness.
What the Fathers know of hearts
   Others can but guess.

Last my heart returned to me
        Such a shining thing,
I could feel its loveliness.
        I could hear it sing.

So wistful little-girl hearts
        Searching for the others
Dull and ache and glow again,
        Finding out the Fathers.

—STELLA WESTON

Reprinted by permission of the author and of *The New York Times*.

*

A DAUGHTER'S LOVE

A happy father thou, when sturdy sons
        In mellowing age a golden youth renew,
In them thy name through generations runs,
        By them achieved, thy early dreams come true.

But happier he whose daughters round him twine
        Their loving arms in his declining years,
And if he smile, their eyes with gladness shine,
        Or if he grieve, their cheeks are wet with tears.

For deeper tenderness hath woman's heart
        For him she loves than son for sire can feel;
His waning hours she cheers with simple art
        And o'er his couch a fragrant breath doth steal

From gentle lips whence no reproaches come,
And a fond breast where thought of self is dumb.

—WILLIAM DUDLEY FOULKE

From *Earth's Generations Pass,* by William Dudley Foulke.
Published by the Oxford University Press, and reprinted by their
permission.

*

COMRADES

Come out! oh, little comrade of the tresses flying free,
Rejoicing in the sunlight that was made for you and me!
To tarry is a folly and to worry is a sin;
Our boat is on the river and the tide comes in.

What roads were ever fairer than the gipsy trails we love,
The mossy rock beneath us and the flying cloud above?
We mock the squirrel's chatter and the calling of the
        crows,
Our feet are on the mountains and the West Wind blows.

The snow-encumbered forest rims a frost-enchanted mere,
The hills are sharp in shadow and the moon is bold and
        clear;
Your cheek is rich in roses that the touch of Winter
        brings;
The lake is frozen midnight and the bright skate rings.

But when we're done with roving under heaven's mighty
        dome,

A deeper joy is waiting in our bounded realm of Home;
My bosom is a pillow for a sunny little head—
It's cozy by the hearthside when the flame glows red.

—ARTHUR GUITERMAN

From *Mirthful Lyre,* by Arthur Guiterman. Copyright, 1918, by
Harper & Brothers.

*

TO MY DAUGHTER

My child, thou seest, I am content to wait.
    So be thou too; with calm secluded mind:
Happy? ah no! nor e'er with hope elate,—
    But still resigned!

Be humbly good, and lift a blameless brow.
    As morning pours the sunlight in the skies,
Suffer, my child, thy sunnier spirit glow
    Through azure eyes!

Victorious, happy, is none in this world's strife.
    Time unto all a fickle lord doth prove;
And Time's a shadow, and, child, our little life
    Is made thereof.

All men, alas! grow weary by the way.
    For to be happy—O fate unkind!—to all
All's lacking. And, though all were granted, say
    What thing so small!

And yet this little thing with anxious care
    Is sought for ceaselessly, by good and vile:

A little gold, a word, a name to wear,
    A loving smile!

The mightiest king o'er love and joy is powerless;
    Vast deserts yearn for but one drop of rain.
Man is a well spring brims, till summer, showerless,
    Makes void again.

Behold these kings of thought we divinize,—
    These heroes, brows transcendent over night,
Names at whose clarion-sound most sombre skies
    Flash lightning-bright!

When once they have fulfilled their glorious doom,
    Earth for awhile a little brighter made,
They find, for all reward, within the tomb
    A little shade.

Kind heaven, that knows our struggles and our sorrows,
    Hath pity on our days, sonorous, vain,
Bathing with tears bright dawn of all our morrows
    Whose noon is pain.

God lightens aye the path whereon we go;
    Still what He is, what we are, brings to mind;
One law revealed in all things here below,
    As in mankind!

That steadfast law, bright-established above,
    On every soul its heavenly beams lets fall:—
Hate nothing, O my child, but all things love,
    Or pity all!

                —Victor Hugo
        Translated by Nelson R. Tyerman

THE CHILD TO THE FATHER

Father, it's your love that safely guides me,
  Always it's around me, night and day;
It shelters me, and soothes, but never chides me:
  Yet, father, there's a shadow in my way.

All the day, my father, I am playing
  Under trees where sunbeams dance and dart—
But often just at night when I am praying
  I feel this awful hunger in my heart.

Father, there is something—it has missed me;
  I've felt it through my little days and years;
And even when you petted me and kissed me
  I've cried myself to sleep with burning tears.

To-day I saw a child and mother walking;
  I caught a gentle shining in her eye,
And music in her voice when she was talking—
  Oh, father, is it *that* that makes me cry?

Oh, never can I put my arms around her,
  Or never cuddle closer in the night;
Mother, oh, my mother! I've not found her—
  I look for her and cry from dark to light!
                              —ROBERT BRIDGES

From *Bramble Brae,* by Robert Bridges. Copyright, 1902, by
Charles Scribner's Sons.

MOTHERLESS

"I wish she had not died," she said;
    The words were soft and low;
"Most little girls like me, papa,
    Have dear mammas, you know.

"There's Lulu Hart next door. Oh, dear!
    I think it is so sweet
To have your mother nod to you
    Across the window-seat.

"And often when we're playing games,
    Lu throws a kiss up there;
And when she rolls her hoople well,
    She knows some one will care.

"Do you think God was good to take
    My own mamma away?
For I was just a baby then—
    Papa, why don't you say?"

"Yes, yes, my child," he sobbed. "Mamma
    Is very happy, dear."
His little girl sprang up, nor cared
    Another word to hear.

"Why, papa, crying! Please don't cry.
    Do you feel sorry, too?
Now, papa, see. I never meant
    I didn't care for you.

"Poor eyes! all wet. I'll kiss them dry.
    What's in your pocket? See.

Oh, where's your watch? Now, won't you please
      Just make it tick for me?

"It's nice to have a dear papa;—
      How big it is, and bright!
I hear it *ticky, ticky, tick!*
      It's *very* loud to-night.

"Ride me to Banbury Cross, papa!
      Now don't you let me fall.
When I was littler, how I slipped!
      I couldn't keep on at all.

"Oh, there's the tea-bell! Now you've tossed
      My hair like everything!
I'll toss yours, too. Oho! oho!
      You look just like a king—

"For kings have crowns, you know, papa,
      And your hair's standing straight.
I knew you'd laugh. There, now, you're good—
      Come, quick, and show Aunt Kate."

Aunt, at the table, glanced at one,
      Then, slyly, at the other;
She could not think what hidden thing
      Had happened to her brother.

His shining hair stood like a crown,
      His smile was warm and bright,—
"Why, John," she said, "you really seem
      Like your old self to-night."

                         —MARY MAPES DODGE

FATHER TO DAUGHTER

I hope there is a little boy somewhere
Who some day will adore your shining hair.

I hope there is a little boy so brave
He won't be frightened when you stamp and rave—

So gentle and so loving he will be
As good to you as I could ever be—

So clever he will see you're far more clever,
So wise that he will never bore you—never.

I hope there is a happy boy and true
Who some day will decide to marry you,

And when he comes to talk to me about it,
I hope I'll like him—but, my dear, I doubt it!

—MIMI

From *Second Conning Tower Book* (*The World,* New York).
Copyright, 1927, by Vanguard Press, Inc.

*

THE CHILD IN THE HOUSE

When from the tower, like some big flower,
The bell drops petals of the hour,
    That says, "It's getting late,"
For nothing else on earth I care
'Cept wash my face and comb my hair,

And hurry out to meet him there,—
  My father at the gate.

It's—oh, how slow the hours go!
  How hard it is to wait!
Till, drawing near, his step I hear,
And up he grabs me, lifts me clear
  Above the garden gate.

        .   .   .   .

—MADISON CAWEIN

From *The Poet and Nature and the Morning Road*, by Madison Cawein. Copyright, 1914, by John P. Morton & Company, Louisville, Ky.

*

A DADDY LIKE MINE

Oh, I worried a lot (and what father has not?)
  That our house was a little bit queer.
It's a roof from the rain, but old-fashioned and plain,
  For it's sheltered us many a year;
And the house is so small there's no parlor at all,
  Just a living-room pleasant and bright,
Just a place where we play at the end of the day
  When we gather together at night.

Once a rich little girl, with her hair all a-curl,
  Came to visit our own little lass,
And she talked of the things only wealth ever brings,
  Of the mansion you glimpse as you pass.
Then I feared that our own, who no riches had known,
  Would be wishing our house were as fine;

But she lifted her head, our wee daughter, and said,
    "But have you got a daddy like mine?"

Yes, I worried, I guess, that I didn't possess
    All the wealth that a mortal can win,
But I worry no more, though so humble our door,
    For I know there are riches within.
There's a fortune of old that is greater than gold,
    It's a fortune that always will do,
If your children are glad, little lass, little lad,
    That their dad is a daddy like you.

                    —DOUGLAS MALLOCH

From *Heart Content,* by Douglas Malloch, copyrighted by the
author and reprinted with his permission.

*

AN "IF" FOR GIRLS

(With apologies to Mr. Rudyard Kipling)

If you can dress to make yourself attractive,
    Yet not make puffs and curls your chief delight;
If you can swim and row, be strong and active,
    But of the gentler graces lose not sight;
If you can dance without a craze for dancing,
    Play without giving play too strong a hold,
Enjoy the love of friends without romancing,
    Care for the weak, the friendless and the old;

If you can master French and Greek and Latin,
    And not acquire, as well, a priggish mien,

If you can feel the touch of silk and satin
    Without despising calico and jean;
If you can ply a saw and use a hammer,
    Can do a man's work when the need occurs,
Can sing when asked, without excuse or stammer,
    Can rise above unfriendly snubs and slurs;
If you can make good bread as well as fudges,
    Can sew with skill and have an eye for dust,
If you can be a friend and hold no grudges,
    A girl whom all will love because they must;

If sometime you should meet and love another
    And make a home with faith and peace enshrined,
And you its soul—a loyal wife and mother—
    You'll work out pretty nearly to my mind
The plan that's been developed through the ages,
    And win the best that life can have in store,
You'll be, my girl, the model for the sages—
    A woman whom the world will bow before.

                    —ELIZABETH LINCOLN OTIS

From *Poems Teachers Ask For*, Book 2, Copyright, by F. A.
Owen Publishing Co., Dansville, N. Y.

*

TO MY LITTLE DAUGHTER

Across the grass I see her pass,
    She walks with stately grace;
A winsome little brown-haired lass,
    With rose-buds in her face.

Fairest of all fair flowers that grow—
    A lily, pure and white;
The one fond treasure that I know,
    Most perfect in my sight.

My every joy—I hold it true—
    In you must find a part;
You are the sunlight breaking through
    The winter of my heart.

                  —E. J. FRANCIS DAVIES

From *Welsh Poets,* edited by A. G. Prys Jones. Copyright, 1917,
by Erskine Macdonald, Ltd.

*

OF A SMALL DAUGHTER WALKING OUTDOORS

Easy, wind!
Go softly here!
She is small
And very dear.

She is young
And cannot say
Words to chase
The wind away.

She is new
To walking, so,
Wind, be kind
And gently blow.

On her ruffled head,
On grass and clover.
Easy wind . . .
She'll tumble over!

—FRANCES M. FROST

Reprinted by permission of the author and the *Delineator*.

*

THE BLACKBIRD

In the far corner
close by the swings,
every morning
a blackbird sings.

His bill's so yellow,
his coat's so black,
that he makes a fellow
whistle back.

Ann, my daughter,
thinks that he
sings for us two
especially.

—HUMBERT WOLFE

From *The Chapbook*, London, and reprinted by permission of *The Living Age*, New York, in which it later appeared.

THE CHILDREN'S HOUR

Between the dark and the daylight,
    When the night is beginning to lower,
Comes a pause in the day's occupations,
    That is known as the Children's Hour.

I hear in the chamber above me
    The patter of little feet,
The sound of a door that is opened,
    And voices soft and sweet.

From my study I see in the lamplight,
    Descending the broad hall stair,
Grave Alice, and laughing Allegra,
    And Edith with golden hair.

A whisper, and then a silence:
    Yet I know by their merry eyes
They are plotting and planning together
    To take me by surprise.

A sudden rush from the stairway,
    A sudden raid from the hall!
By three doors left unguarded
    They enter my castle wall!

They climb up into my turret
    O'er the arms and back of my chair;
If I try to escape, they surround me;
    They seem to be everywhere.

They almost devour me with kisses,
    Their arms about me entwine,

Till I think of the Bishop of Bingen
    In his Mouse-Tower on the Rhine!

Do you think, O blue-eyed banditti,
    Because you have scaled the wall,
Such an old mustache as I am
    Is not a match for you all!

I have you fast in my fortress,
    And will not let you depart,
But put you down into the dungeon
    In the round-tower of my heart.

And there will I keep you forever,
    Yes, forever and a day,
Till the walls shall crumble to ruin,
    And moulder in dust away!
           —HENRY WADSWORTH LONGFELLOW

From *Poetical Works of Henry Wadsworth Lonfellow*. Used by permission of, and by special arrangement with, Houghton Mifflin Company, the authorized publishers.

*

LOST CHILD

The Little Girl that I used to know—
Tell me, what can have gone with her,
Here she was, but a jiff ago—
All my yesterdays shone with her.
Tiny feet that I taught to walk—
Wavering first little steps to me;
Balancing, laughing, eyes aglow,

Proud and safe when she caught my knee.
Baby lips that I tuned to talk—
How the dimples beset her so!
'Who is this that I sort o' found,
Pattering, puttering, projecking 'round?'
'Papa's Comfy, that's who I be!'

Tall and straight as a sapling spruce,
Now over Daddy's head she sees.
But can she fathom the mysteries
Daddy hugs in a tired old heart?
What can she measure of 'What's the use'?
How can she know what herself she means—
Half-way immortality lent;
All the tenderness, all the smart—
To the Grizzled Chum of Before She Went,
Prophet that loved her Before She Came?
New thoughts flutter, and other scenes
Beckon her—and I cannot blame.
But only one thing in the world's the same,
Never shaken and never spent—
Daddy's love for the babe she Meant,
Love for whatso she e'er can be;
Change, nor Sorrow, nor very Shame
Can hide my child from me.

Leave her, best, to her own device,
Let her follow her conscious feet,
Wilful now, they can go alone
For the paths of Youth are sweet,
And Life must school its own.
And Daddy can Wait.
Some day, sure as the homing bird,
Sure as the sun on the glacier's ice,

Safe as Sorrow and Fixed as Fate—
Some day so shall her heart be stirred
And a dumb old man that waits afar
Shall hear the little feet—and a Word
'Why, Daddy! And here we are!'

Come she proudly, or come she bent,
Queen or outcast, of flushed or grey—
Time is only—Another Day;
Love—that it may be lent.
She will be but my babe again;
All behind and between shall be
Naught and naught as a dream of pain—
When she stands again at my knee.

—CHARLES FLETCHER LUMMIS

From *Bronco Pegasus,* by Charles Fletcher Lummis. Used by permission of, and by special arrangement with, Houghton Mifflin Company, the authorized publishers.

*

TO DORIS

How weak those dear, uncertain hands
Held with spread fingers, baby-wise;
And how their helpless quest commands
Such service as no master buys!

What do you seek, my darling? Toys?
The red fish? the green frog? the blue
Rabbit, whose color-scheme destroys
No whit the gravity in you?

Take them. You scarce can hold them yet . . .
But can a grown-up father hold
His toys more firmly? No, my pet;
His grasp too falters, uncontrolled.

Ah, would that he might feel, how near!
A loving Father with kind eyes
And patient hands, how firm to steer
Weak, wavering fingers toward their prize.

Could he thus feel, he would not dread
Days he must dream of, when no more
Green frog, blue rabbit, fish of red,
Will be the toys you hanker for:

Days when, a woman grown, you long
For love, for beauty, for delight . . .
And find your arms, that seem so strong,
Too frail to guard them from the night.

—LEE WILSON DODD

From *The Great Enlightenment,* by Lee Wilson Dodd. Copyright,
1928, by Harper & Brothers.

TO MY DAUGHTER

Concerning a bunch of blossoms

The blossoms she gave him—indeed, they were fair;
And grateful the odor they cast on the air;
And he put them in water, and set them anigh

His little round window that looked on the sky.
And the blush of those blossoms, their pleasant perfume,
Made a sweet little spot in that dull little room—
Made a sweet little spot for a day and an hour;
Then—
   Well, little Lil what's the fate of a flower?

The blossoms she gave him—indeed, they were fair;
But I think that the least of the giving was there,
In that vase by the window—the look in her face—
Her tender and youthful and delicate grace—
The voice that just trembled in gentle replies,
The look and the light in her uplifted eyes—
Ah! these to my thinking were dearer by far
Than ever the fairest of May-blossoms are.

The blossoms she gave him—you ask, little Lil,
With a lip that is quivering and blue eyes that fill—
If they faded?
   They did—but there's no need to cry!
For they blossomed again where I can't have them die—
These roseate tints on your soft little cheek,
In a manner mysterious certainly speak
Of a bunch of pink blossoms, fresh torn from the tree,
That in eighteen-and-eighty your mother gave me.

     —H. C. BUNNER

From *Poems*, by H. C. Bunner. Copyright, 1917, by Charles Scribner's Sons.

BEING A DAUGHTER

Being a daughter's not an easy thing—
  The sort of daughter that I'd like to be:
Unselfish, patient, always quick to bring
  The comfort needed; keen enough to see
The longings hard to guess at, and fulfill them,
The lonelinesses and the fears, and still them.

Being a daughter's not an easy thing—
  I've always really wanted my own way.
And so it's hard to keep remembering
  That what seems right and good to us today,
To older minds brings horror and alarm,
Although it may not have a bit of harm!

Being a daughter's not an easy thing—
  Putting aside rebellion, eagerness;
For, though some days I long to have my fling,
  I know that the old path of loveliness,
Of quietness and calm, sweet dignity,
Is better than those roads more gay to see.

Being a daughter's not an easy thing—
  The sort of daughter that I'd like to be:
To share my rose, keep to myself the sting,
And show a face of calm serenity;
Being a daughter—it's a task severe,
But it's my favorite choice of a career!

—Mary Carolyn Davies

From *Ladies' Home Journal,* and reprinted by permission of the author.

DAUGHTERS

I know I never did devise
Two tall girls with kind clear eyes.
This is more than life allows:
Two tall girls with candid brows.
I wonder how one understands
Two tall girls with slim, deft hands,
Quiet, graceful, moved to mirth
By—to them—a smiling earth.

Children that they were I've known.
Now, they hardly seem my own.
Now a sudden stride is taken
And the bough of life is shaken
Musical for them; for me
'Tis a gnarled, deep-rooted tree
Flourishing through sun and rain
From the darkest soil of pain.

Can it be they move and breathe
With anything I could bequeath?
Most their mother, yet not she,
Strangely they have come to be
Two tall girls who unaware
Waken spring in winter air
And with their beauty say "Let be!"
To all straitened agony.

I know I never did devise
In love and passion on this wise.
She, all grace, conceived this grace.
Yet in time and out of space
An individual pulse and thought

Have clearly and distinctly wrought
Some stilly miracle made new
In the difference of these two.

—WILLIAM ROSE BENÉT

From *The New Republic,* and reprinted by permission of the author.

*

A FAREWELL

My fairest child, I have no song to give you;
    No lark could pipe in skies so dull and gray;
Yet, if you will, one quiet hint I'll leave you,
    For every day.

I'll tell you how to sing a clearer carol
    Than lark who hails the dawn or breezy down;
To earn yourself a purer poet's laurel
    Than Shakespeare's crown.

Be good, sweet maid, and let who can be clever;
    Do lovely things, not dream them, all day long;
And so make Life, and Death, and that For Ever,
    One grand sweet song.

—CHARLES KINGSLEY

From *Poems,* by Charles Kingsley. Copyright, 1902. By permission of The Macmillan Company, publishers.

*

BEQUEST TO MY DAUGHTERS

Though it grieve you,
This is all that
I shall leave you:

White and slender
Buoyant bodies,
Which will gender

Love and wonder;
Beauty newer
Than leaves under

April's flashing
Silver rainfalls
And their splashing.

To the youngest
I leave dreaming;
To the strongest

Streams for leaping,
Trees to be like,
Shade for sleeping;

Something singing
In the other
Like the winging

Panegyric
Of a swallow—
Some deep lyric

Pride of living.
That is all I
Shall be giving.

—LAWRENCE LEE

From *Virginia Quarterly Review,* and reprinted by permission of the author.

MARY WHITE

This tribute to his daughter, Mary, was written by William Allen White on the day of her funeral, and was printed the following day in *The Emporia Gazette*.

The Associated Press reports carrying the news of Mary White's death declared that it came as the result of a fall from a horse. How she would have hooted at that! She never fell from a horse in her life. Horses have fallen on her and with her—"I'm always trying to hold 'em in my lap," she used to say. But she was proud of few things, and one was that she could ride anything that had four legs and hair. Her death resulted not from a fall, but from a blow on the head which fractured her skull, and the blow came from the limb of an overhanging tree on the parking.

The last hour of her life was typical of its happiness. She came home from a day's work at school, topped off by a hard grind with the copy on the High School Annual, and felt that a ride would refresh her. She climbed into her khakis, chattering to her mother about the work she was doing, and hurried to get her horse and be out on the dirt roads for the country air and the radiant green fields of the spring. As she rode through the town on an easy gallop she kept waving at passers-by. She knew every one in town. For a decade the little figure with the long pigtail and the red hair ribbon has been familiar on the streets of Emporia, and she got in the way of speaking to those who nodded at her. She passed the Kerrs, walking the horse, in front of the Normal Library, and waved at them; passed another friend a few hundred feet further on, and waved at her. The horse was walking and as she turned into North Merchant Street she took off her cowboy hat, and the horse swung into a lope. She passed the Tripletts and waved her cowboy hat at them, still moving gaily north on Merchant Street. A *Gazette* carrier passed —a High School boy friend—and she waved at him, but with her bridle hand; the horse veered quickly, plunged into the parking where the low-hanging limb faced her, and, while she still looked back waving, the blow came. But she did not fall from the horse; she slipped off, dazed a bit, staggered and fell in a faint. She never quite recovered consciousness.

But she did not fall from the horse, neither was she riding fast. A year or so ago she used to go like the wind. But that habit was broken, and she used the horse to get into the open to get fresh, hard exercise, and to work off a certain surplus energy that welled up in her and needed a physical outlet. That need has been in her heart for years. It was back of the impulse that kept the dauntless, little brown-clad figure on the streets and country roads of this community and built into a strong, muscular body what had been a frail and sickly frame during the first years of her life. But the riding gave her more than a body. It released a gay and hardy soul. She was the happiest thing in the world. And she was happy because she was enlarging her horizon. She came to know all sorts and conditions of men; Charles O'Brien, the traffic cop, was one of her best friends. W. L. Holtz, the Latin teacher, was another. Tom O'Connor, farmer-politician, and Rev. J. H. J. Rice, preacher and police judge, and Frank Beach, music master, were her special friends, and all the girls, black and white, above the track and below the track, in Pepville and Stringtown, were among her acquaintances. And she brought home riotous stories of her adventures. She loved to rollick; persiflage was her natural expression at home. Her humor was a continual bubble of joy. She seemed to think in hyperbole and metaphor. She was mischievous without malice, as full of faults as an old shoe. No angel was Mary White, but an easy girl to live with, for she never nursed a grouch five minutes in her life.

With all her eagerness for the out-of-doors, she loved books. On her table when she left her room were a book by Conrad, one by Galsworthy, *Creative Chemistry* by E. E. Slosson, and a Kipling book. She read Mark Twain, Dickens, and Kipling before she was ten—all of their writings. Wells and Arnold Bennett particularly amused and diverted her. She was entered as a student in Wellesley in 1922; was assistant editor of the High School Annual this year, and in line for election to the editorship of the Annual next year. She was a member of the executive committee of the High School Y.W.C.A.

Within the last two years she had begun to be moved by an ambition to draw. She began as most children do by scribbling in her school books, funny pictures. She bought cartoon magazines and took a course—rather casually, naturally, for she was, after all, a child, with no strong purposes—and this year she tasted the first fruits of success by having her pictures accepted by the High School Annual. But the thrill of delight she got when Mr. Ecord, of the Normal Annual, asked her to do the cartooning for that book this spring was too beautiful for words. She fell to her work with all her enthusiastic heart. Her drawings were accepted, and her pride—always repressed by a lively sense of the ridiculousness of the figure she was cutting—was a really gorgeous thing to see. No successful artist ever drank a deeper draught of satisfaction than she took from the little fame her work was getting

among her schoolfellows. In her glory, she almost forgot
her horse—but never her car.

For she used the car as a jitney bus. It was her social
life. She never had a "party" in all her nearly seventeen
years—wouldn't have one; but she never drove a block
in the car in her life that she didn't begin to fill the car
with pick-ups! Everybody rode with Mary White—white
and black, old and young, rich and poor, men and women.
She liked nothing better than to fill the car full of long-
legged high-school boys and an occasional girl, and parade
the town. She never had a "date," nor went to a dance,
except once with her brother, Bill, and the "boy proposi-
tion" didn't interest her—yet. But young people—great,
spring-breaking, varnish-cracking, fender-bending, door-
sagging carloads of "kids"—gave her great pleasure. Her
zests were keen. But the most fun she ever had in her life
was acting as chairman of the committee that got up the
big turkey dinner for the poor folks at the county home;
scores of pies, gallons of slaw, jam, cakes, preserves,
oranges, and a wilderness of turkey were loaded in the
car and taken to the county home. And being of a prac-
tical turn of mind, she risked her own Christmas dinner
by staying to see that the poor folks actually got it all.
Not that she was a cynic; she just disliked to tempt folks.
While there she found a blind colored uncle, very old,
who could do nothing but make rag rugs, and she rustled
up from her school friends rags enough to keep him busy
for a season. The last engagement she tried to make was
to take the guests at the county home out for a car ride.
And the last endeavor of her life was to try to get a rest
room for colored girls in the high school. She found one
girl reading in the toilet, because there was no better place
for a colored girl to loaf, and it inflamed her sense of
injustice and she became a nagging harpy to those who

she thought could remedy the evil. The poor she had always with her, and was glad of it. She hungered and thirsted for righteousness; and was the most impious creature in the world. She joined the Congregational Church without consulting her parents; not particularly for her soul's good. She never had a thrill of piety in her life, and would have hooted at a "testimony." But even as a little child she felt the church was an agency for helping people to more of life's abundance, and she wanted to help. She never wanted help for herself. Clothes meant little to her. It was a fight to get a new rig on her; but eventually a harder fight to get it off. She never wore a jewel and had no ring but her High School class ring, and never asked for anything but a wrist watch. She refused to have her hair up, though she was nearly seventeen. "Mother," she protested, "you don't know how much I get by with, in my braided pigtails, that I could not with my hair up." Above every other passion of her life was her passion not to grow up, to be a child. The tom-boy in her, which was big, seemed to loathe to be put away forever in skirts. She was a Peter Pan, who refused to grow up.

Her funeral yesterday at the Congregational Church was as she would have wished it; no singing, no flowers save the big bunch of red roses from her Brother Bill's Harvard classmen—Heavens, how proud that would have made her! and the red roses from the *Gazette* force—in vases at her head and feet. A short prayer, Paul's beautiful essay on "Love," from the Thirteenth Chapter of First Corinthians, some remarks about her democratic spirit by her friend, John H. J. Rice, pastor and police judge, which she would have deprecated if she could, a prayer sent down for her by her friend, Carl Nau, and opening the service the slow, poignant movement from Beethoven's Moonlight Sonata, which she loved, and closing the service a cutting from the joyously melancholy first movement of Tschaikowski's Pathetic Symphony, which she liked to hear in certain moods on the phonograph; then the Lord's Prayer by her friends in the High School.

That was all.

For her pallbearers only her friends were chosen; her Latin teacher, W. L. Holtz; her high-school principal, Rice Brown; her doctor, Frank Foncannon; her friend, W. W. Finney; her pal at the *Gazette* office, Walter Hughes; and her brother Bill. It would have made her smile to know that her friend, Charley O'Brien, the traffic cop, had been transferred from Sixth and Commercial to the corner near the church to direct her friends who came to bid her good-by.

A rift in the clouds in a gray day threw a shaft of sunlight upon her coffin as her nervous, energetic little body sank to its last sleep. But the soul of her, the glowing, gorgeous, fervent soul of her, surely was flaming in eager joy upon some other dawn.

—WILLIAM ALLEN WHITE

From *The Emporia Gazette,* and reprinted by permission of the author.

IV

FOR FATHERS TO ENJOY

RESPONSIBLE WILLIAM

"Yes, sir!" says Willy, "I was wild!
But it does sober up a child
To have to show his parents how
A fellow should be brought up now.

"I have to show ma how to win me
And help the old man discipline me;
I tell you it is no child's play
To train the parents of to-day."

—KEITH PRESTON

From *Pot Shots from Pegasus,* by Keith Preston. Copyright, 1929, by Covici, Friede Inc.

*

THE CRIB

I sought immortality
    Here and there—
I sent my rockets
    Into the air:
I gave my, name
    A hostage to ink;
I dined a critic
    And bought him drink.

I spurned the weariness
    Of the flesh;

161

Denied fatigue
    And began afresh—
If men knew all,
    How they would laugh!
I even planned
    My epitaph . . .

And then one night
    When the dusk was thin
I heard the nursery
    Rites begin:
I heard the tender
    Soothings said
Over a crib, and
    A small sweet head.

Then in a flash
    It came to me
That there was my
    Immortality!

        —CHRISTOPHER MORLEY

From *The Rocking Horse,* by Christopher Morley. Copyright, 1919, by Doubleday, Doran and Company, Inc.

*

APPLE AND ROSE

My little daughter is a tea-rose,
Satin to the touch,
Wine to the lips,
And a faint, delirious perfume.

But my little son
Is a June apple,
Firm and cool,
And scornful of too much sweetness,
But full of tang and flavor
And better than bread to the hungry.

O wild winds and clumsy, pilfering bees,
With the whole world to be wanton in,
Will you not spare my little tea-rose?
And O ruthless blind creatures,
Who lay eggs of evil at the core of life,
Pass by my one red apple,
That is so firm and sound!

—KARLE WILSON BAKER

From *Blue Smoke,* by Karle Wilson Baker. Copyright, 1919, by Yale University Press, and reprinted by their permission.

*

TO A VERY YOUNG GENTLEMAN

Dear Stranger: Let me welcome you
    To this sublunar region.
May your adversities be few,
    And your delights be legion.

Men call our world a vale of tears,
    Both farcical and fearful,
Though I believe in after years
    You'll find it rather cheerful.

No doubt you will be much surprised
    At many things you see here;
But, if our hopes are realized,
    You will be glad to be here.

Since you are come to live with men,
    I trust that you will find us
Agreeable and polite; and when
    We're not, you mustn't mind us.

You'll have a time with safety-pins
    And baptism and teething,
And Love and Sentiment and Sins
    As natural as breathing.

You'll have to learn your A B C's,
    Your Creed and Catechism
And "duty toward," and out of these
    Unravel your own "ism."

You'll have to learn the use of flame,
    The friendship of cold water,
Don't be afraid; just play the game,
    And never cry for quarter.

You'll get the best of circumstance
    By working like a beaver.
And when you meet with True Romance
    Be sure you never leave her.

—BLISS CARMAN

From *The Woman's Home Companion*. Reprinted by permission of Dodd, Mead & Company, Inc.

THE CHILD'S PLAY OF MEN

It must be fun like dad to play
   In his big store down town,
To have a lot of games all day,
   And never stop to frown:
To measure yards of everything,
   And weigh big things and small,
To hear the voice of traffic sing,
   And prices rise and fall.

For that is all dad has to do,
   As far as I can see,
If St. Augustine's word is true
   That mother told to me.
"For children's play," Augustine said,
   "When they are grown to men,
Is children's play, though earning bread,
   They call it business then."
            —MICHAEL EARLS, S. J.

From *Ballads of Childhood,* by Michael Earls, S. J. Copyright, 1912, by Benziger Brothers, and reprinted by their permission.

*

PARENTAL RECOLLECTIONS

A child's a plaything for an hour;
   Its pretty tricks we try
For that or for a longer space;
   Then tire, and lay it by.

But I knew one, that to itself
   All seasons could control;

That would have mock'd the sense of pain
  Out of a grieved soul.

Thou straggler into loving arms,
  Young climber up of knees,
When I forget thy thousand ways,
  Then life and all shall cease.

—CHARLES LAMB

From *Childhood in Verse and Prose,* edited by S. Miles. Copyright, 1923, by Oxford University Press.

*

FIRST TROUSERS

Little man, little man,
  With your little trousers blue,
I wish that I were happy,
  My little man, like you.
Is there ever anything in life
  That gives such pleasure true
As this first pair of trousers,
  So stunning and so new?

Little man, little man,
  You with sturdy stride and bold,
Pray, have you seen my baby boy?
  He passed this way, I'm told.
His little dress is fresh and white,
  His clustering curls are gold—
He's naught else but a baby,
  For he's but three years old!

Little man, little man,
    Why, can it really be?
When I ask if you've seen him,
    You say that you are he?
You, with your stride and trousers,
    And magic pockets three?
'Tis quite hard to believe it,
    You look so strange to me.

          —SUSIE DAWSON BROWN

From *Good Cheer Book,* edited by B. E. Herbert. Copyright, 1919, by Lothrop, Lee, & Shepard Co.

*

'ROUND FATHER'S GRIP

When Father's come from some long trip
We chicks all kneel around his grip
And try to keep our faces straight
And not look tickled while we wait
Till he has hugged our mother tight
And kissed her twice with all his might.
We're glad to see him, too, but then
First thing when he's got home again
From some great long and busy trip
We want to see what's in his grip!

Then Father kneels among us there
And digs a key-ring from somewhere
And looks as if he had forgot
To bring us things—we know he's not!
We gather close while he unlocks

The grip. Then each one gets a box
Or parcel tied up with a string
Or some such gifty-looking thing
That's 'zactly right. We squeal: "Oh, Dad!
The nicest things we've ever had!"

It's not just what we get, you see,
That makes us glad. For it might be
If Father came home once without
The gifts for us we'd give a shout
And hug him hard. But oh, it's great
That when he's in some other State
'Way off from home he thinks of us,
From ten-year Blanche to one-year Gus,
So when he's come home from his trip
We kneel and giggle 'round his grip!

—STRICKLAND GILLILAN

From *Including You and Me,* by Strickland Gillilan. Copyright,
1916, by Forbes & Co.

WHEN DAD TAKES ME

My dad sometimes some little trip
        Takes me along—and, my, it's fun!
He puts my (you know) in his grip,
        A suit (not this, my Sunday one),
And other things that Mother, too,
Says I will need. (I never do.)

I'd always rather go with dad
        Than go with her. (Oh, goodness me,

Of course I love her, course I'm glad
 That she's my mother—as can be.)
But when my mother lets me go
With dad!—well, lots of things, you know.

For instance, Father doesn't scrub
 Me night and day and all the time.
My mother keeps me in a tub
 And says it really is a crime
How dirty children (me she means)
Can get, no matter how one cleans.

But Father, huh, he doesn't care,
 Ask "How's your neck?" or "How's your ears?"
Or worry what you have to wear,
 Or if a button disappears,
Dad doesn't watch you day and night
And say you simply are a fright.

Then we get home. "Just see that child,"
 My mother says, "as black as ink!
I knew you'd leave him running wild.
 My goodness, what will people think!
You'll never take—my, my, these men!—
That boy, with my consent, again."

      —Douglas Malloch

A CONSISTENT ANTI TO HER SON

You're twenty-one to-day, Willie,
    And a danger lurks at the door,
I've known about it always,
    But I never spoke before;
When you were only a baby
    It seemed so very remote,
But you're twenty-one to-day, Willie,
    And old enough to vote.

You must not go to the polls, Willie,
    Never go to the polls,
They're dark and dreadful places
    Where many lose their souls;
They smirch, degrade and coarsen,
    Terrible things they do
To quiet, elderly women—
    What would they do to you!

If you've a boyish fancy
    For any measure or man,
Tell me, and I'll tell Father,
    He'll vote for it, if he can.
He casts my vote, and Louisa's,
    And Sarah, and dear Aunt Clo;
Wouldn't you let him vote for you?
    Father, who loves you so?

I've guarded you always, Willie,
    Body and soul from harm;
I'll guard your faith and honor,
    Your innocence and charm

From the polls and their evil spirits,
    Politics, rum and pelf;
Do you think I'd send my only son
    Where I would not go myself?

                    —ALICE DUER MILLER

*

PARENTHOOD

The birches that dance on the top of the hill
Are so slender and young that they cannot keep still,
They bend and they nod at each whiff of a breeze,
For you see they are still just the children of trees.

But the birches below in the valley are older,
They are calmer and straighter and taller and colder.
Perhaps when we've grown up as solemn and grave,
We, too, will have children who do not behave!

                    —JOHN FARRAR

*

PORTRAIT OF A CHILD

Unconscious of amused and tolerant eyes,
    He sits among his scattered dreams, and plays.
    True to no one thing long; running for praise
With something less than half begun. He tries

To build his blocks against the furthest skies.
    They fall; his soldiers tumble; but he stays
    And plans and struts and laughs at fresh dismays—
Too confident and busy to be wise.

His toys are towns and temples; his commands
    Bring forth vast armies trembling at his nod.
He shapes and shatters with impartial hands . . .
And, in his crude and tireless play, I see
    The savage, the creator, and the god:
All that man was and all he hopes to be.

                              —Louis Untermeyer

From *These Times,* by Louis Untermeyer. Copyright, by Harcourt,
Brace and Company, Inc.

                              *

WHEN I WAS ONE-AND-TWENTY

When I was one-and-twenty
    I heard a wise man say,
"Give crowns and pounds and guineas
    But not your heart away;
Give pearls away and rubies
    But keep your fancy free."
But I was one-and-twenty,
    No use to talk to me.

When I was one-and-twenty
    I heard him say again,
"The heart out of the bosom
    Was never given in vain;

'Tis paid with sighs a plenty
    And sold for endless rue."
And I am two-and-twenty,
    And oh, 'tis true, 'tis true.

—A. E. HOUSMAN

From *The Shropshire Lad,* by A. E. Housman. Reprinted by courtesy of the author.

*

HOW NO AGE IS CONTENT

Laid in my quiet bed, in study as I were,
I saw within my troubled head a heap of thoughts appear.
And every thought did shew so lively in mine eyes,
That now I sigh'd, and then I smiled, as cause of thought
    did rise.
I saw the little boy in thought how oft that he
Did wish of God, to scape the rod, a tall young man to be.
The young man eke that feels his bones with pains opprest,
How he would be a rich old man, to live and lie at rest.
The rich old man that sees his end draw on so sore,
How he would be a boy again, to live so much the more.
Whereat full oft I smiled, to see how all these three,
From boy to man, from man to boy, would chop and
    change degree.

.   .   .   .

—HENRY HOWARD, EARL OF SURREY

From *Poems,* by Henry Howard, Earl of Surrey. Copyright, by Bell & Daldy.

ON THE BIRTH OF A SON

by Su Shih, also called Su Tung-Po (1036-1101 A.D.)

Families when a child is born
Hope it will turn out intelligent.
I, through intelligence
Having wrecked my whole life,
Only hope that the baby will prove
Ignorant and stupid.
Then he'll be happy all his days
And grow into a cabinet minister.

—ARTHUR WALEY, *Translator*

From *170 Chinese Poems,* by Arthur Waley, Translator. By permission of, and special arrangement with, Alfred A. Knopf, Inc., authorized publishers.

THIRST

Every little
    While all day
I am thirsty,
    And I say
To anybody
    Who is nigh,
"I want a drink."

Every little
    While all night
I wake up, and
    I am quite

Thirsty. And I
  Softly cry,
"I want a drink."

Father says if
  I should go
Up to Heaven,
  They would know
Me because I
  Am so dry,
"I want a drink."

—RALPH BERGENGREN

*

HEADACHE JES' 'FORE SCHOOL

I guess my health is gittin' poor,
    Er somep'ner the kin'
For every mornin' jist as sure
    (Especially if it's fine)
I git sich offul pains
    'At ma says: "It's jes' cru'l
Ter make 'at boy study with
    Such headaches jes' 'fore school."

Ma thinks my mind is breakin' down
    From learnin' of so much.
She puts wet towels on my head,
    An' chopped up ice, an' such,

An' tries ter git me off ter bed,
But pa says he's no fool,
He thinks birch oil's the only stuff
Fer headaches jes' 'fore school.

An' teacher, too, don't symp'thize
'Ith boys wot's feelin' bad,
Fer, soon's she sees me mopin' in,
She says: "Now ain't 'at sad
Ter make them suff'rin' children work!
Young man, set on 'at stool
An' do them sums." Huh! she makes fun
Of headaches jes' 'fore school.

'Tis kind'r funny, though, how soon
I'm over bein' sick,
An' me an' Jim (Jim, he gits cramps),
We sneak off down t' the crick
An' go in swimmin'. Gee! We got
A bully divin' pool
An' spring board. Gosh! you bet they cure
Them headaches jes' 'fore school.

An' fishin', too. We got a raft
An' dandy hooks an' lines,
Ketch bullheads, lots—an' sunfish. Say!
Down underneath them pines
They bite like thunder! Settin' there,
Feet swashin', nice an' cool.
Pains, nothin'! Say, d' you ever git
Them headaches jes' 'fore school?

—MAURICE C. JOHNSON

From *Good Cheer Book*, edited by B. E. Herbert. Copyright, 1919, by Lothrop, Lee, & Shepard Company.

REPROVE GENTLY

He who checks the child with terror,
    Stops its play and stills its song,
Not alone commits an error,
    But a grievous moral wrong.

Would you stop the flowing river,
    Thinking it would cease to flow?
Onward must it flow forever—
    Better teach it *where to go.*

—ANONYMOUS

From *One Hundred Choice Selections.* Used by permission of
and arrangement with The Penn Publishing Company, Philadelphia.

*

SONG AGAINST CHILDREN

O the barberry bright, the barberry bright!
It stood on the mantelpiece because of the height.
Its stems were slender and thorny and tall
And it looked most beautiful against the grey wall.
But Michael climbed up there in spite of the height
And he ate all the berries off the barberry bright.

O the round holly wreath, the round holly wreath!
It hung in the window with ivy beneath.
It was plump and prosperous, spangled with red,
And I thought it would cheer me although I were dead.
But Deborah climbed on a table beneath
And she ate all the berries off the round holly wreath.

O the mistletoe bough, the mistletoe bough!
Could anyone touch it? I did not see how.
I hung it up high that it might last long,
I wreathed it with ribbons and hailed it with song.
But Christopher reached it, I do not know how,
And he ate all the berries off the mistletoe bough.

—ALINE KILMER

From *Vigils,* by Aline Kilmer. Copyright, 1921, by Doubleday, Doran and Company, Inc.

*

IN DEFENSE OF CHILDREN

Though parents think their children rude,
Especially about their food,

And call their table manners low,
I really have not found them so.

I never yet have known a boy,
From Skaneateles to Troy,

From Sacramento to New York,
Who took his porridge with a fork;

Nor any girl beneath the moon
Who managed mince-pie with a spoon;

Nor any child, in all my life,
That ate its ice-cream with a knife!

—ARTHUR GUITERMAN

From *Mirthful Lyre,* by Arthur Guiterman. Copyright, 1918, by Harper & Brothers.

BOYS

Now if any one has an easy time
    In this world of push and pull,
It is not the boy of the family,
    For his hands are always full.
I'd like to ask who fills the stove?
    Where is the girl that could?
Who brings in water, lights the fire,
    And splits the kindling wood?

And who is it that cleans the walks
    After hours of snowing?
In summer who keeps down the weeds
    By diligently hoeing?
And who must harness the faithful horse,
    When the girls would ride about?
And who must clean the carriage?
    The boy, you'll own, no doubt.

And who does the many other things
    Too numerous to mention?
The boy is the "general utility man,"
    And really deserves a pension!
Friends, just praise this boy sometimes,
    When he does his very best;
And don't always want the easy chair
    When he's taking a little rest.

Don't let him always be the last
    To see the new magazine;
And sometimes let the boy be heard,
    As well as to be seen.
That boys are far from perfect,
    Is understood by all;

But they have hearts, remember,
　For "men are boys grown tall."

And when a boy has been working
　His level best for days,
It does him good, I tell you,
　To have some hearty praise.
He's not merely a combination
　Of muddy boots and noise,
And he likes to be looked upon
　As one of the family joys.

　　　　　—ANONYMOUS

From *Good Cheer Book,* edited by B. E. Herbert. Copyright, 1919,
by Lothrop, Lee, & Shepard Co.

*

PA'S SOFT SPOT

"All folks hev some soft spot,"
　Ma uster say,
"Somethin' or 'nother
　Comes out some day
Comes out 'fore they know it,
　Jest like ez not."
'N'en us kids'd say, "Ma,
　What's your sof' spot?"

An' we'd keep a plaguin',
　Till ma'd say,
"I wish 'at you youngins
　'D run away!
Ask your pa' bout his'n
　An', like ez not,

He'll tell you willin'ly
    What's his sof' spot."

'N'en we'd 'gree to ask him
    That very day;
When his train'd whistle
    Why right away,
We'd jest skedaddle
    Clean 'cross the lot,
To be first to ask pa
    What's his sof' spot.

Pa, he'd say, "My sof' spot?
    Never hes none!"
Wouldn't tell us neither,
    But jest make fun;
Then he'd tell his brakeman,
    He'd say "Great lot,
Think you're goin' to tell 'em
    What's your sof' spot!"

'N'en we'd all go home,
    An' after 'while
Pa'd tell ma 'bout it,
    An' ma she'd smile;
We'd 'gin agin a guessin',
    Till pa'd say, "Trot!
Time you kids wuz dreamin'
    In some sof' spot."

An' pa'd never tell us,
    When he wuz in;
Ev'ry trip he come home
    We'd 'gin agin;

Onct George sez when prayin',
    He prayed a lot,
"Please God, wisht you'd tell us
    What's pa's sof' spot!"

One day the opurat'r
    Sent word by Bert
There hed bin a washout,
    An' pa wuz hurt;
Engineer wuz hurt, too,
    An' both might die;
Pa wanted to see us
    To say good-by.

We wuz all so still
    When we went in;
They wuz holdin' pa up,
    A fannin' him;
An' pa sez "I may die
    Jest like ez not,
Tell the children I sed
    They's my sof' spot!"

But our pa didn't die,
    He jist got well;
We wuz all so happy,
    Couldn't 'gin to tell!
'Cause we all loved our pa,
    A great big lot,
I guess God saw we wuz
    Pa's sof' spot!

—D. A. Ellsworth

From *One Hundred Choice Selections*. Used by permission of and arrangement with The Penn Publishing Company, Philadelphia.

LITTLE MAMMA

Why is it the children don' love me
    As they do mamma?
That they put her ever above me—
    "Little mamma?"
I'm sure I do all that I can do,
What more can a rather big man do,
    Who can't be mamma—
        Little mamma?

Any game that the tyrants suggest,
"Logomachy,"—which I detest,—
Doll-babies, hop-scotch, or baseball,
I'm always on hand at the call.
When Noah and the others embark,
I'm the elephant saved in the ark.
I creep, and I climb, and I crawl—
By turns am the animals all.
        For the show on the stair
        I'm always the bear,
The chimpanzee, or the kangaroo.

        It is never, "Mamma,—
            Little mamma,—
        Won't you?"

My umbrella's the pony, if any—
None ride on Mamma's parasol:
I'm supposed to have always the penny
For bon-bons, and beggars, and all.
My room is the one where they clatter—
Am I reading, or writing, what matter!
My knee is the one for a trot,

My foot is the stirrup for Dot.
If his fractions get into a snarl
Who straightens the tangles for Karl?
Who bounds Massachusetts and Maine,
And tries to bound flimsy old Spain?
      Why,
    It is I,
      Papa,—
Not little mamma!

That the youngsters are ingrates don't say.
I think they love me—in a way—
As one does the old clock on the stair,—
Any curious, cumbrous affair
That one's used to having about,
And would feel rather lonely without.
I think that they love me, I say,
In a sort of a tolerant way;
    But it's plain that papa
    Isn't little mamma.

Thus when shadows come stealing anear,
And things in the firelight look queer;
When shadows the play-room enwrap,
They never climb into my lap
And toy with *my* head, smooth and bare,
As they do with mamma's shining hair;
Nor feel round my throat and my chin
For dimples to put fingers in;
Nor lock my neck in a loving vise,
And say they're "mousies"—that's mice—
    And will nibble my ears,
    Will nibble and bite
With their little mice-teeth, so sharp and so white.

If I do not kiss them this very minute—
Don't-wait-a-bit-but-at-once-begin-it—
    Dear little papa!
That's what they say and do to mamma.

If, mildly hinting, I quietly say that
Kissing's a game that more can play at,
They turn up at once those innocent eyes,
And I suddenly learn to my great surprise
    That my face has "prickles"—
    My moustache tickles.
If, storming their camp, I seize a pert shaver,
And take as a right what was asked as a favor,
    It is, "O papa,
    How horrid you are—
You taste exactly like a cigar!"

But though the rebels protest and pout,
And make a pretence of driving me out,
I hold, after all, the main redoubt,—
Not by force of arms nor the force of will,
But the power of love, which is mightier still.
And very deep in their hearts, I know,
Under the saucy and petulant "oh,"
The doubtful "yes," or the naughty "no,"
    They love papa.

And down in the heart that no one sees,
Where I hold my feasts and my jubilees,
I know that I would not abate one jot
Of the love that is held by my little Dot
Or my great big boy for their little mamma,
Though out in the cold is crowded papa.
I would not abate it the tiniest whit,

And I am not jealous the least little bit;
For I'll tell you a secret: Come, my dears,
And I'll whisper it—right-in-to-your-ears—
    I, too, love mamma,
    Little mamma!

            —CHARLES HENRY WEBB

From *Poetry of American Wit and Humor,* edited by Knowles.

               *

TO A BOY, WITH A WATCH

Is it not sweet beloved youth,
    To rove through Erudition's bowers,
And cull the golden fruits of truth,
    And gather Fancy's brilliant flowers?

And is it not more sweet than this,
    To feel thy parents' hearts approving,
And pay them back in sums of bliss
    The dear, the endless debt of loving?

It must be so to thee, my youth;
    With this idea toil is lighter;
This sweetens all the fruits of truth,
    And makes the flowers of Fancy brighter!

The little gift we send thee, boy,
    May sometimes teach thy soul to ponder,
If indolence or siren joy
    Should ever tempt that soul to wander;

'Twill tell thee that the winged day
 Can ne'er be chain'd by man's endeavour;
That life and time shall fade away,
 While heaven and virtue bloom for ever!

      —THOMAS MOORE

From *Poetical Works,* by Thomas Moore. Copyright, by Frederick
Warne & Co.

*

LITTLE BILLY

The Doctor came at half-past one,
 Little Billy saw him from the window.
The Doctor he was short and fat,
He hid a trumpet in his hat,
And spoke with his ear. You may all doubt that,
 But little Billy saw it from the window.

The Doctor left at half-past four,
 Little Billy saw him from the window.
The Doctor's head was white and bare,
Like an ostrich egg in a nest of hair,
The marble bounced right up in the air
 When little Billy dropped it from the window.

The Doctor came with a small black bag,
 Little Billy saw it from the window.
And what do you think he had in that?
Why, a great big howling, yowling brat,
With a voice like a discontented cat.
 Little Billy heard it from the window.

And that's how the new brother came,
   While little Billy waited at the window.
"Who would have thought that Brother Jack
Would yell like that! They ought to pack
Him into the bag and send him back,"
   Said angry little Billy at the window.
                    —SIR ARTHUR CONAN DOYLE

*

LITTLE WILLIE'S HEARING

Sometimes w'en I am playin' with
   some fellers 'at I knows,
My ma she comes to call me, 'cause she
   wants me, I surpose:
An' then she calls in this way: "Willie!
   Willie, dear! Willee-e-ee!"
An' you'd be surprised to notice how
   dretful deef I be;
An' the fellers 'at are playin' they
   keeps mos' orful still,
W'ile they tell me, just' in whispers:
   "Your ma is callin', Bill."
But my hearin' don't git better, so fur
   as I can see,
W'ile my ma stan's there a-callin':
   "Willie! Willie, dear! Willee-e-ee!"

An' soon my ma she gives it up, an'
   says: "Well, I'll allow

It's mighty cur'us w'ere that boy has
    got to, anyhow;
An' then I keep on playin' jus' the way
    I did before—
I know if she was wantin' much she'd
    call to me some more.
An' purty soon she comes agin an'
    says: "Willie! Willee-e-ee!"
But my hearin's jus' as hard as w'at it
    useter be.
If a feller has good judgment, an' uses
    it that way,
He can almos' allers manage to git
    consid'ble play.

But jus' w'ile I am playin', an' prob'ly
    I am "it,"
They's somethin' diff'rent happens, an'
    I have to up, an' git,
Fer my pa comes to the doorway, an'
    he interrup's our glee;
He jus' says, "William Henry!" but
    that's enough fer me.
You'd be surprised to notice how
    quickly I can hear
W'en my pa says, "William Henry!"
    but never "Willie, dear!"
Fer though my hearin's middlin' bad to
    hear the voice of ma,
It's apt to show improvement w'en the
    callin' comes from pa.

—ANONYMOUS

From *Normal Instructor and Primary Plans.*

PAPA AND THE BOY

Charming as is the merry prattle of innocent childhood, it is not particularly agreeable at about one o'clock in the morning. There are young and talkative children who have no more regard for your feelings or for the proprieties of life than to open their eyes with a snap at one or two in the morning, and to seek to engage you in enlivening dialog of this sort.

"Papa!"

You think you will pay no heed to the imperative little voice, hoping that silence on your part will keep the youngster quiet; but again that boy of three pipes out sharply:

"Papa!"

"Well?" you say.

"You 'wake, papa?"

"Yes."

"So's me."

"Yes, I hear that you are," you say with cold sarcasm. "What do you want?"

"Oh! nuffin."

"Well, lie still and go to sleep then."

"I isn't s'eepy, papa."

"Well, I am, young man."

"Is you? I isn't—not a bit. Say, papa, papa! If you was wich what would you buy me?"

"I don't know—go to sleep."

"Wouldn't you buy me nuffin?"

"I guess so; now you—"

"What, papa?"

"Well, a steam engine, maybe; now you go right to sleep."

"With a bell that would ring, papa?"

"Yes, yes; now you—"

"And would the wheels go wound, papa?"

"Oh! yes (yawning). Shut your eyes now, and—"

"And would it go choo, choo, choo, papa?"

"Yes, yes; now go to sleep."

"Say, papa."

No answer.

"Papa!"

"Well, what now?"

"Is you 'fraid of the dark?"

"No" (drowsily).

"I isn't either. Papa!"

"Well?"

"If I was wich I'd buy you somefin."

"Would you?"

"Yes; I'd buy you some ice-cweam and some chocolum drops and a toof brush and panties wiv bwaid on like mine, and a candy wooster, and—"

"That will do. You must go to sleep now."

Silence for half a second, then—

"Papa! Papa!"

"Well, what now?"

"I want a jink."

"No, you don't."

"I do, papa."

Experience has taught you that there will be no peace until you have brought the "jink," and you scurry out to the bathroom in the dark for it, knocking your shins against everything in the room as you go.

"Now I don't want to hear another word from you to-night," you say, as he gulps down a mouthful of the water he didn't want. Two minutes later he says:

"Papa!"

"See here, laddie, papa will have to punish you if—"

"I can spell 'dog,' papa."

"Well, nobody wants to hear you spell at two o'clock in the morning."

"B-o-g—dog; is that right?"

"No, it isn't. But nobody cares if—"

"Then it's d-o-g, isn't it?"

"Yes, yes; now you lie right down and go to sleep instantly."

"Then I'll be a good boy, won't I, papa?"

"Yes; you'll be the best boy on earth.   Good night, dearie."

"Papa!"

"Well, well! What now?"

"Is I your little boy?"

"Yes, yes; of course."

"Some mans haven't got any little boys; but you have, haven't you?"

"Yes."

"Don't you wish you had two, free, nine, 'leben, twenty-six, ninety-ten, free hundred little boys?"

The mere possibility of such a remote and contingent calamity so paralyzes you that you lie speechless for ten minutes during which you hear a yawn or two in the little bed by your side, a little figure rolls over three or four times, a pair of heels fly into the air once or twice, a warm, moist little hand reaches out and touches your face to make sure that you are there, and the boy is asleep with his heels where his head ought to be.

—J. L. HARBOUR

From *Humorous Bits and How to Hold an Audience*, edited by G. Kleiser. Copyright, 1908, by Funk & Wagnalls.

TO MY CHILDREN

Almighty God grants you this wondrous life
To use in aid of His great purposes . . .
You shall not then devote your time and toil
Nor give your heart to selfish power and gain;
But, striving to attain a worthy goal,
So live that with a retrospective gaze
Your eyes fall not upon a darkened course
Obscured by wrecks of others' joys and hopes,
But find a path made beautiful and bright
With blossoms of your love and generous aid.

So live, that when your final hour comes
Your anxious thought will search the bygone years
To justify your lives unto yourself.
Sad be your fate if then you learn—too late
That all of self alone must die with you;
For only what you have for others done
Will live, to mark the limits of your worth.

—JOHN J. BURCHENAL

From *Collier's*.

*

THE CANE-BOTTOM'D CHAIR

In tattered old slippers that toast at the bars,
And a ragged old jacket perfumed with cigars,
Away from the world and its toils and its cares,
I've a snug little kingdom up four pair of stairs.

To mount to this realm is a toil, to be sure,
But the fire there is bright and the air rather pure;
And the view I behold on a sunshiny day
Is grand through the chimney-pots over the way.

This snug little chamber is cramm'd in all nooks
With worthless old nicknacks and silly old books,
And foolish old odds and foolish old ends,
Crack'd bargains from brokers, cheap keepsakes from
    friends.

Old armour, prints, pictures, pipes, china (all crack'd),
Old rickety tables, and chairs broken-backed;
A twopenny treasury, wondrous to see;
What matter? 'tis pleasant to you, friend, and me.

No better divan need the Sultan require,
Than the creaking old sofa that basks by the fire;
And 'tis wonderful, surely, what music you get
From the rickety, ramshackle, wheezy spinet.

That praying-rug came from a Turcoman's camp;
By Tiber once twinkled that brazen old lamp;
A Mameluke fierce yonder dagger has drawn:
'Tis a murderous knife to toast muffins upon.

Long, long through the hours, and the night, and the
    chimes,
Here we talk of old books, and old friends, and old times;
As we sit in a fog made of rich Latakie
This chamber is pleasant to you, friend, and me.

But of all the cheap treasures that garnish my nest,
There's one that I love and I cherish the best:

For the finest of couches that's padded with hair
I never would change thee, my cane-bottom'd chair.

. . . . .

—WILLIAM MAKEPEACE THACKERAY

*

CHILD IN THE GARDEN

When to the garden of untroubled thought
    I came of late, and saw the open door,
    And wished again to enter, and explore
The sweet, wild ways with stainless bloom inwrought,
And bowers of innocence with beauty fraught,
    It seemed some purer voice must speak before
    I dared to tread that garden loved of yore,
That Eden lost unknown and found unsought.

Then just within the gate I saw a child,—
    A stranger-child, yet to my heart most dear;
He held his hands to me, and softly smiled
    With eyes that knew no shade of sin or fear:
"Come in," he said, "and play awhile with me;
I am the little child you used to be."

—HENRY VAN DYKE

HERO WANTED

A boy's heart is a light heart,
    A true heart, a clean heart.
A boy's heart is a *right* heart
    If it has half a chance;
It's leal and kind and tender
    A knightly and a keen heart
That glows with fire and splendor
    And thrills with high romance!

A boy's way is a lithe way,
    A brave way, a strong way,
He takes his gay and blithe way
    Amid the worldly throng
A-seeking for adventure
    And if he goes the wrong way
Not his should be the censure
    But those who lead him wrong.

A boy loves strength and vigor
    Of mind and of sinew
He wants life braver, bigger
    With more of zest and joy.
You must be fine and real
    And give the best that's in you
If you'd be friend, ideal,
    And Hero to a boy!

—BERTON BRALEY

From *Hurdy-Gurdy on Olympus,* by Berton Braley. Copyright, 1927, by D. Appleton & Company, and reprinted by their permission.

FOR THE BIRTHDAY OF A MIDDLE-AGED CHILD

I'm sorry you are wiser,
   I'm sorry you are taller;
I liked you better foolish,
   And I liked you better smaller.
I'm sorry you have learning
   And I hope you won't display it;
But since this is your birthday
   I suppose I mustn't say it.

I liked you with your hair cut
   Like a mediaeval page's,
And I hate to see your eyes change
   From a seraph's to a sage's.
You are not half so beautiful
   Since middle-age befell you;
But since this is your birthday
   I suppose I mustn't tell you.

—ALINE KILMER

From *Selected Poems,* by Aline Kilmer. Copyright, 1929, by
Doubleday, Doran and Company, Inc.

*

THE GRADUATING CLASS

In a bank of flowers, against a wall of roses, they stand,
They in whom our lives have flowered.
A flutter of excitement is in them, like a wind in the
   garden, tossing their heads and swaying their firm
   young necks.

The songs and the speeches, the lights and the lookers-on,
    rise in them like quick sap.

But we who watch them are still—and full of questions.
There is so much that we could give them, so little they
    can take.
Our knowledge is a mist in their eyes, a tarnish on the
    golden fruit.

Outside of Eden a chill comes down.
Twenty feet of space, laden with the scent of roses, is
    wide as the years, sharp as the flaming sword.
Only, because we love them, hope struggles a little against
    knowledge.
The wind of adolescence stirs their hearts and sways their
    firm young necks—
And our throats ache with tenderness.

—E<small>UNICE</small> T<small>IETJENS</small>

From *Profiles from Home,* by Eunice Tietjens. By permission
of, and special arrangement with Alfred A. Knopf, Inc., authorized
publishers.

THE MISCREANT, ANGEL

To L. S., Jr.

Angel Cadotte was mischievous, more roguish
Than any chipmunk in a bin of oats.
But when the daily storm of wrath would break
After a prank upon the priest or teacher,
And justice—in the form of Michael Horse,
The reservation policeman—sought to lay

A rod of birch across his quivering back,
Angel would scurry to my side for refuge,
And cling tenaciously upon my legs
Until the storm had passed—as any woodsman,
Buffeted, beaten by tumultuous rains,
Seeks out the shelter of a thick-boughed fir,
And flattening himself against the trunk,
Clings to the bark with fingers desperate.

Oh, it was good to be a friendly fir-tree
Shielding a wild young body from the storm;
And good to feel the frenzied clutch of hands,
The cannonading of a wild young heart.
And if, in the fancy of a luckless wildling,
You were the only fir-tree in the world
That had a lee and overhanging boughs,
What would you do? And did you ever see
A tree, offended by some childish prank,
Fold up its branches? walk away in wrath?
And leave a little boy without a shelter
Against the beat of rain? Impossible!

—Lew Sarett

From *Slow Smoke,* by Lew Sarett. Copyright, 1925, by Henry Holt and Company, and reprinted by permission of the author and publishers.

*

LOOKING BACK

By *"Deacon Green"*

If I were a boy again,—ah, me!—
How very, very good I'd be!
I would not sulk, I would not cry,

I'd scorn to coax for cake or pie.
I would not cause Mamma distress,
I'd never hate to wash and dress.
I'd rather learn a task than play,
And ne'er from school I'd run away.
I'd any time my jack-knife lend,
And share my toys with every friend.
I'd gladly go to bed at six,
And never be "as cross as sticks."
I'd run with joy to take a pill,
And mustard wear whenever ill.
I'd never wish to skate or swim,
But wisely think of dangers grim.
And, oh, I'd never, just for fun,
Beg to go hunting with a gun!
At every naughty thing I did—
For mischief might be somewhere hid—
I'd drop at once upon my knees,
And say, "Dear Teacher, flog me, please."

It's easy to be good, you see,
When looking back from sixty-three.

—MARY MAPES DODGE

From *Rhymes and Jingles,* by Mary Mapes Dodge. Copyright, 1927, by Charles Scribner's Sons.

*

THE OLD BOYS

What are the youngsters saying—
    We, who have played so long,
Now should be done with playing?
    Why, we are going strong!

Who stumped the handicappers?
    Who stroked the record crew?
We'll show the whippersnappers
    More than a trick or two!

Youth is a bit too heady,
    Rash in the glow of dawn.
Trained are our nerves and steady;
    Brain is a match for brawn.

And if our pace is slowing,
    There is a lot in knack;
Yes, and a lot in knowing.
    Who says we can't come back?

Say we are much too sporty,
    Say what you wish and will;
Call us too old at forty,
    Fifty shall find us still

Trying the same old races,
    Winning the same old holes,
Scoring the same old aces,
    Shooting the same old goals.

—ARTHUR GUITERMAN

FATHER, WHERE DO THE WILD SWANS GO?

Father, where do the wild swans go?
    Far, far. Ceaselessly winging,
    Their necks outstraining, they haste them singing
    Far, far. Whither, none may know.

Father, where do the cloud-ships go?
    Far, far. The winds pursue them,
    And over the shining heaven strew them
    Far, far. Whither, none may know.

Father, where do the days all go?
    Far, far. Each runs and races—
    No one can catch them, they leave no traces—
    Far, far. Whither, none may know.

But father, we—where do we then go?
    Far, far. Our dim eyes veiling,
    With bended head we go sighing, wailing
    Far, far. Whither none may know.

—Ludwig Holstein

Translated by Charles Wharton Stork

From *Poetry: A Magazine of Verse,* and with the permission of the translator.

INDEX OF TITLES

Printed in the USA
CPSIA information can be obtained
at www.ICGtesting.com
LVHW092315250224
772790LV00005B/176

9 781406 704983